M000105625

MINDFULNESS FOR THERAPISTS

Mindfulness for Therapists: Practice for the Heart encourages therapists to embrace mindfulness practice to create presence and depth in their work with clients. Mindfulness helps therapists cultivate compassion, relieve stress, and weather the often emotionally difficult work of providing therapy. In addition, the therapist's own meditation practice is a necessary foundation for teaching mindfulness to clients. Through a variety of exercises and stories from his own clinical experience, McCollum helps therapists understand the usefulness of mindfulness and develop their own practice.

Eric E. McCollum, PhD, is Professor and Program Director of the Marriage and Family Therapy Master's Program at Virginia Tech, where he teaches mindfulness meditation to his students in the Marriage and Family Therapy training program. He has practiced psychotherapy for nearly 40 years and has practiced meditation in the Buddhist *vipassana* tradition for more than 30 years.

MINDFULNESS FOR THERAPISTS

Practice for the Heart

Eric E. McCollum

Routledge
Taylor & Francis Group

NEW YORK AND LONDON

First published 2015
by Routledge
711 Third Avenue, New York, NY 10017

and by Routledge
27 Church Road, Hove, East Sussex BN3 2FA

*Routledge is an imprint of the Taylor & Francis Group,
an informa business*

© 2015 Taylor & Francis Group

The right of Eric E. McCollum to be identified as the author of this
Work has been asserted by him in accordance with sections 77 and
78 of the Copyright, Designs and Patents Act 1988.

Library of Congress Cataloging-in-Publication Data

McCollum, Eric E., author.
  Mindfulness for therapists : practice for the heart / Eric McCollum.
    p. ; cm.
  Includes bibliographical references and index.
  I. Title.
[DNLM: 1. Mindfulness.   2. Psychotherapy—methods.
3. Burnout, Professional—prevention & control.   4. Self Care—
psychology. WM 420]
  RC480.5
  616.89'14—dc23
  2014014313

ISBN: 978-0-415-89826-3 (hbk)
ISBN: 978-1-138-80587-3 (pbk)
ISBN: 978-1-315-75193-1 (ebk)

Typeset in Sabon
by Apex CoVantage, LLC

Printed and bound in the United States of America by Publishers Graphics,
LLC on sustainably sourced paper.

CONTENTS

CONTENTS

PREFACE

In the past, when I've written a book, it's because I've believed that I've come to the end of something. A book seems to be the chance to set out definitively what you think you know. This book is different. Rather than a report from the end of a journey, it's more like a lengthy letter written along the way. I don't think of it that way because I don't think I know anything. I do. But mindfulness practice—the subject of this book—isn't something that has an end. It is a challenging journey that can last a lifetime if we choose to let it. Each time I've thought maybe I was near the end, there's always another hill ahead that I'm irresistibly drawn to climb to see what's on the other side.

I'd like you to think of this book, then, as an invitation. I truly believe, and my experience bears out, that mindfulness practice can be an invaluable part of being a therapist. I'll make the case in depth later in the book, but in brief, mindfulness helps us with many of the things about being a therapist that are hard or that get in our way. It helps with stress. It helps us be present. It helps us find the common humanity we share with our clients, so that our empathy and connection with them is genuine. It's a road I've been traveling for a number of years now and I'd like to invite you to travel it with me. It isn't always an easy road, and it certainly isn't a superhighway, but there certainly are rewards along the way.

I decided to write this book because I kept seeing in the professional literature the recommendation that if therapists planned to use mindfulness in their work with clients, it was important that they have their own mindfulness practice. I wholeheartedly agree with that recommendation. Basic meditation instructions are pretty simple and easy to give. That isn't where the skill and experience come in. Therapists need their own mindfulness practice to deal with what comes after you've given the instructions. That's when the hard work begins. That's when it's important to be able to discern when clients are on the right path or when they are losing the way. While conceptual frameworks help with that discernment, experience is the final touchstone. Sometimes this practice takes us to difficult and scary places. Sometimes it gives us pleasures that seem like the end of the road when they're not. Knowing in our own bones how that feels makes us much more able to help clients as they encounter the same things. And when it comes down to it, I'm really not going to encourage you to try teaching your clients the formal practice of mindfulness, at least not often and not much. I think the real benefit of this practice for therapists is what it does for us both personally and professionally. We help our clients by bringing our own best selves into the therapy room, and mindfulness helps us do that more consistently and fully.

This is a book for practicing therapists and for students who are beginning the professional journey to become therapists. Despite all the recommendations I was hearing about the importance to therapists having their own practice, I didn't find much direction for how to do so that was aimed specifically at therapists. There are lots and lots of good books about mindfulness and meditation and compassion but none focused on how those practices apply to the needs and lives of therapists. So I decided that was the book I was going to write. Why me? I've had a mindfulness practice in the insight meditation or *vipassana* tradition since the early 1980s. My practice has ebbed and flowed but has been part of my life since I was first exposed to it while a staff member at the Menninger Clinic. We were lucky enough to have a skilled practitioner and teacher—Dr. Jack Engler—on the staff who began to teach the practice and organize sitting groups. I honestly don't know what drew me to meditation at that time. I guess it was some sense that life could be different for me, that some of the struggles I was engaged in could be untangled.

My practice ran parallel to my professional life, or so it seemed to me, for many years. Now we have the topic of mindfulness everywhere— on magazine covers, in television shows, in scientific papers, and in the self-help aisle at the bookstore. Mindfulness is taught in universities and public school and to preschoolers. As I write this, there is even a member of Congress—Ohio Representative Tim Ryan—who wants to bring mindfulness to the entire country. It wasn't always so. When I first began to meditate, I recall feeling that it was a bit suspect, a little clandestine. I didn't tell many people that I meditated. And I certainly didn't tell anyone when I went to my first meditation retreat. Who would understand why I would choose to spend 5 days in the woods with a group of strangers, not talking to any of them, not even making eye contact, and meditating from 5 in the morning until 10 at night? Using meditation in therapy seemed like a risky and questionable thing to do.

In this book, I'll talk about Buddhist psychology. This isn't an attempt to convince anyone to take up Buddhist religion. The insights of the historical Buddha as they have been developed and passed down over the past 2,500 years can be useful to us without adopting the religious aspects of Buddhism. In fact, what the Buddha taught was much more like a philosophy or psychology than it was like a religion. The religious

PREFACE

aspect became part of Buddhism only later as it spread throughout India and encountered other religions and spiritual practices.

One aspect of Buddhist psychology that I find useful is the Three Refuges. These are supports for spiritual development and the practice of mindfulness. One of those refuges is called the *sangha* or the community. None of us can really get far in this practice all by ourselves. For me, as a therapist, I began to feel the influence of the community when I started to see the initial studies that explored the usefulness of mindfulness in helping to treat a variety of disorders. The courage of early pioneers like Jon Kabat-Zinn helped to bring this practice into our field. His lead was followed by a growing cadre of researchers and practitioners who are continuing to expand the reach of mindfulness in health care and mental health care. Others are taking it to education. Perhaps it will even make it into our government one of these days.

I took a training workshop from Jon Kabat-Zinn and his colleague Saki Santorelli in Mindfulness-Based Stress Reduction almost 20 years ago now. It gave me a beginning vision of how this practice might become part of my professional work. Slowly, I began to talk with my colleagues about my meditation experience and how I thought it might be useful. I offered a 1-day workshop to the students and faculty in the marriage and family therapy program that I now direct. To my surprise, a lot of people attended. Also to my surprise, my colleagues were supportive. I began to hold informal meditation sessions after class for those who wanted more experience with the practice. I started attending retreats to deepen my own practice and found a wonderful teacher—Tara Brach of the Insight Meditation Community of Washington. With further support of my colleagues, I began to formally teach mindfulness to our students as they began their clinical training. The response was enthusiastic. I developed and taught a full course on mindfulness. We held day-long retreats and organized a monthly sitting group. At this point, we have truly integrated mindfulness into the curriculum of our program. Not long ago, I got a note from a recent graduate who had just completed a 6-week silent mindfulness meditation retreat. She wrote how much the experience had meant to her and how much she had gained from it. "This never would have happened without mindfulness being such an integral part of the MFT program," she said.

So I am inviting you along on the same journey as I have made, and my students have made, and generations of people before us have made. Some days when I sit down to meditate, I feel the presence of all of those people, of that *sangha*, around me. I am trying really hard not to say it takes a village. But it certainly is a lonely path if you are all alone.

So many people have helped me along the way that I want to take a moment to thank some of them. Jack Engler first taught me mindfulness at Menninger along with my colleagues Bill Trussell, Marianne

ix

Ault-Riche, Peter Novotny, and Cecil Chamberlain. These people were all part of a regular sitting group that met weekly in the morning before work, and they helped get the ball rolling. Tara Brach has been an incredible influence, both for her teaching and for her manner in the world. She has been an informal consultant to us as we have integrated mindfulness into our training program and has had a profound impact on my personal practice as well. My colleagues Dr. Sandi Stith and Dr. Karen Rosen created an atmosphere at Virginia Tech where I felt safe to begin to talk about my experience and they encouraged me to pursue integrating it into our program even when they didn't exactly understand what I was up to. My current colleagues have continued that support. Dr. Angela Huebner and Kirsten Lundeberg have been amazingly good friends and colleagues along the way. I was lucky enough to have a talented editor and writer—Faye Fiore—help edit sections of the book. My wife Julia Stephens has put up with taking care of all my responsibilities while I sat retreats and has never questioned why I would or should pursue this practice. But in the end I owe the greatest debt to my clients and my students. They have taught me more than they can ever guess about the practice of mindfulness, and about the simple grace of being human.

1

THE CHALLENGE OF PRESENCE
IN A MULTITASKING WORLD

Roger[1] is still on his cell phone as he comes down the hall to my office. His voice is so loud that it is impossible not to overhear.

"Tell them I'll be back in about an hour," he says. There's a pause. "No, I can't be disturbed."

A longer pause this time as Roger listens intently.

"Okay," he says finally. "Tell them to send me an e-mail. Or call if it's really urgent."

As he sits down in my office, Roger is still staring at his phone, swiping his finger across the screen.

"Just a second," he says. "I need to check on one thing."

I sit quietly while he reads e-mail and types quickly with his thumbs. He is clearly checking on more than one thing. He looks up when he is done.

"What a day," he says, looking distracted. "Everyone seems to want a piece of me."

"Just take a moment to leave that all behind," I tell him.

I guide us both through a brief present focus experience that I do with most clients at the beginning of my sessions: taking a conscious breath or two, feeling our feet on the floor, the chair against our body . . . coming into the present.

"Better," Roger says. He begins to tell me about his thoughts since I last saw him, how he struggles with a vague, background sense of anxiety that always leaves him feeling unsettled. He doesn't have panic attacks or frank anxiety symptoms, just a consistent feeling of unease.

As we talk, his cell phone vibrates insistently in his shirt pocket, signaling either an incoming call or an arriving e-mail. We both ignore it as best we can, but finally Roger says, "I guess I better check on that." He looks at the screen and his eyes narrow.

"Damn," he says. "It never stops."

Roger is right. It doesn't stop. The incoming demands for our attention are relentless, compelling, intrusive, stressful, and seductive all at once. And our cell phones are only the most obvious offenders. Wherever we go, we seem to be connected to "the cloud"—computers sit on our

1

desks, iPads ride in our briefcases, and smartphones buzz in our pockets, while cable TV and satellite radios connect us to an unimaginable array of news, entertainment, and . . . distraction. The cloud we are connected to quickly becomes "the crowd" since most incoming bits of information carry interpersonal demands of various kinds. Some demands are direct and insistent: answer my e-mail, take my call. Others are more passive but no less compelling. Television and the Internet bring us a steady stream of images—war, poverty, natural disaster, as well as sex, romance, and beauty—hat all call forth a human response. How are we to manage it all?

It's tempting to think that only our clients suffer from the stresses of multitasking and that therapists remain calm and centered in the midst of the electronic maelstrom. But it isn't so. As Roger's cell phone buzzes in our session, my mind occasionally drifts back to a disturbing e-mail that popped up in my inbox a few minutes before he arrived. My ear is half-cocked for the soft ping of a text message on my phone. I haven't heard from my wife all day and am wondering when she will be able to get away from her office to meet me for dinner. We communicate by text during the day in an effort not to interrupt each other with a phone call, but even the possibility of hearing from her keeps my thoughts a little off center. At the end of our session, I open my iPad to schedule Roger's next appointment. As he is writing a check, I am tempted to quickly check a couple of blogs that I read regularly. And after he leaves, I plunge into the e-mails that accumulated during our session—trying hard to catch up before my next client arrives.

Therapy rooms seem more crowded today than they used to be, even when there are only two people in them. When I came to the Menninger Clinic in the late 1970s as a trainee, I entered therapy with another therapist on the staff. As a psychoanalytic institution, there was a strong tradition at Menninger of personal therapy for those of us in training, and excellent therapists were abundant among the staff. My therapist's office was in the idyllically named White Cottage—an old farmhouse that had been turned into therapy offices. I can still recall how quiet it was sitting in the small waiting room before my appointments, and the sense of refuge I felt in my therapist's office, as though therapy was a chance to take a time out from the world. It would be years before computers would sit on our desks, or blinking voicemail lights would call us, or texts and e-mails come cascading to our cell phones. When sitting in the little waiting room awaiting my therapist, my mind certainly wanted to focus elsewhere at times, but technology had yet to wrap us in the cloud of connection that makes such a deluge of information and connection instantly available and that offers us so many digital superhighways away from the present moment.

It is, of course, tempting to romanticize the past. There were plenty of distractions then, as well. Many of them sprang, as they still do, from the ways our minds work to transport us into the past or future, into worry or regret, anticipation or longing. As I waited for my therapy appointment in White Cottage, my mind could be a hundred different places—replaying past hurts, imagining future pleasures—anywhere but in that small room, feeling the air movement as someone walked past, or feeling the fatigue in my legs from the walk over to the cottage. Mindfulness practice developed over centuries to help us understand and manage the mind's seeming allergy to being present. The temptations of the digital world only provide more tempting and efficient ways for the mind to leave the present moment behind. But their efficiency challenges us even more strongly to preserve the qualities of *presence* and *depth* in our interactions. As therapists, both qualities are essential to our healing work.

Being and Doing as Therapists

What is therapy about, fundamentally? Segal, Williams, and Teasdale (2002)—therapists who use a mindfulness approach to help prevent relapse following a major depressive episode—distinguish between two "modes of mind" in their work that can be illustrative for our discussion. These modes are *doing mode* and *being mode*. Doing mode is what we generally associate with therapy. We *do* a lot of things with our clients— we set goals, plan actions, make interventions, assign between-session tasks, restructure, restory, and reframe, all in the service of helping things change. Doing is goal oriented and designed to change what's there in our lives that isn't satisfying into what we *want* to be there. If the room is cold, we adjust the thermostat. If it's hot, we take off our sweaters. Doing mode is extremely useful. This book would not have been written, published, or distributed without many people operating in doing mode. Were we to abandon doing mode as therapists, our clients would lose much-needed help. However, as my colleague Diane Gehart and I have argued elsewhere (Gehart & McCollum, 2007), relying only on the doing orientation to therapy can side with clients' culturally conditioned belief that if they just *do* more, or different, things that they can finally achieve a state of no suffering. Therapists can fall victim to this belief as well. Much of our training focuses on doing. We are schooled in models of intervention and take workshops to learn new therapeutic techniques. Doing approaches are extraordinarily helpful when our clients bring us discrete situations in which change can be made. But they begin to fall short as clients come to wrestle with the inevitable suffering of life, or when they are not yet ready to take the steps that could provide them relief. We need a counterbalance to doing, a complementary stance. According to Segal and colleagues, that complementary mode of mind is *being*.

What are the qualities of being? Where doing mode is focused on achieving goals and reducing the discrepancies between how life is and how we want it to be, being mode steps away from the driven quality of doing. Segal et al. (2002) describe it this way: "the focus of the being mode is 'accepting' and 'allowing' what is, without any immediate pressure to change it" (p. 73). Being mode also shifts our orientation to time. Where doing is often focused on an imagined or wished-for future, being exists only in the present moment. As mindfulness teachers like to say, "In the present moment, there's nothing to do and nowhere to go."

I first consciously encountered the difference between doing and being modes many years ago—before I even had a name for them. I was with a friend in Charleston, South Carolina, and we had taken a tour boat ride around the harbor. As we came back to the terminal, a sudden thunderstorm struck with lightning and a downpour of rain. We were sheltered under a broad canopy, completely dry, and with a bench to sit on. Perhaps as a result of my growing experience with mindfulness meditation, I was enjoying just watching the rain and the activity of the harbor as boats raced to find shelter. My friend, however, was becoming increasingly agitated.

"What're we going to do?" he said. "We've got to meet our friends in 15 minutes." This was before the days of cell phones, so we didn't have an easy way to contact our buddies, whom we were supposed to meet at a café several blocks away.

"I'm sure they'll figure out what happened," I said. My friend wasn't comforted.

"What if they think we went somewhere else? What if they leave?"

"If nothing else, we'll meet up back at the hotel eventually. Look how you can see the rain coming across the bay. With the sun against it, it looks so deep blue."

My friend glanced quickly at the storm and then began searching his pockets for change.

"Maybe there's a pay phone somewhere," he said. "I'm gonna go look. I can call the restaurant." He went inside the ferry terminal. While he was gone, the sky came alive with an amazing lightning display and rain blew in from the open water in sheets. I was having a great time just watching the storm and enjoying the feeling of security in the shelter of the broad porch. My friend came back.

"No phone," he said. He started pacing back and forth. "Damn."

After a few moments the storm blew through and the sun came out.

"Thank God," my friend said. He was standing in front of me now, facing the wall of the building, urgency in his voice. "Let's go. Jesus, we're late enough already."

Behind him, the sun streamed down through the receding storm clouds in a beautiful display of shadows at play. He missed the view completely.

What brings me back to this experience is the way it illustrates the difference between a doing approach and a being approach. My friend's notion that he had to do something to make the situation conform to what we had planned—to get to the restaurant on time—left him on edge and agitated when he couldn't find a way to make it work. On the other hand, my ability to simply sit and enjoy what presented itself provided a moment of refuge and peace.

I don't want to make too much of our 15 minutes of experience on the harbor in Charleston. I certainly don't meet all seeming adversities with as much equanimity as I did that day, nor is my friend a fundamentally driven person, never able to relax, take a breath, and find joy in the world despite a change in plans. But our reactions do point to the difference between doing and being. And the weather provides us with a good arena for practice because we have no control over it at all. In that regard, it is not unlike many aspects of our inner life—thoughts, moods, physical sensations—all of which come and go on their own, and often with little influence on our part. One of my teachers—Tara Brach—talks about meditation practice as helping us learn to live with our "inner weather"—the emotional thunderstorms, grey days, summer sunsets, cold winters, and lovely spring days—that characterize our inner lives. Through mindfulness practice we come to see that struggling against them leads to suffering while acceptance at least holds the promise of peace.

As therapists, we certainly need the ability to *do* with clients. But we need the ability to *be* as well—the ability to be with our client's pain without having to immediately try to fix what isn't fixable, to be with our client's hesitation to act when rushing it would only heighten their indecision, to let the story unfold in a session as it needs to unfold, not as we'd like it to do so. We need this ability because sometimes the doing mode can actually increase suffering even when our hope is that taking action will reduce the pain.

I had a client a few years ago who experienced a miscarriage in her first pregnancy. She and her husband were anxious to start a family, although they had put it off while they finished graduate school and had a good start on their careers. Like most couples, they were overjoyed to find that she was pregnant, and they were devastated, only a few weeks later, when the pregnancy miscarried. Supported by family and friends, they began to regroup and readjust their lives to a vision of not having the baby they had so eagerly anticipated. I saw her a few weeks later and asked how she was doing.

"It's frustrating," she said. "I'm sad all the time."

"You had a big loss," I said. "Being sad makes sense."

"But it doesn't seem to be getting better," she said. "I should be over it by now."

"What's the timetable you're on?" I asked.

"Everyone says we should try again, but I don't want to . . . I don't feel like it. What if I never want to have a baby?" Tears were running down her cheeks by now.

"I know how frustrating it must feel but maybe you need to be with what's happening and let the process take its course. Sometimes healing takes time."

"But what if I don't have time?" she said. I could hear the fear in her voice. "What if it never gets better? I try to make myself want another baby but I don't. I just don't."

It was tempting as her therapist to suggest an antidepressant, or to dispute her scary thoughts, or to try to *do* something. But I also knew my client to be a very organized and focused young woman whose task-oriented approach to life had finally run into something that wouldn't yield to more effort. Encouraging her to find a new strategy to make things better would likely only add to her suffering. Instead, I helped her sit with the fear and the sadness, talk to her husband (from whom she had been hiding her feelings), and not listen so trustingly to well-meaning friends and family members who suggested she plunge right back into trying to become pregnant. As she gradually learned to stop resisting her experience, and to engage with her feelings of sadness and fear without letting them become overwhelming, they became less frightening and she was able to slowly grieve her loss and begin to have some hope again. She is now a happy and successful mother of two children who continue to teach her daily that life often comes on its terms, not on ours.

Being with difficult experiences is a challenging lesson for all of us to learn, but especially, I think, for Westerners. We have such confidence that anything broken can be fixed, that anything difficult can be eased, that any dilemma can be resolved, or that any answer can be found through Google, that *being* with difficulty, rather than immediately trying to fix things, seems foreign and weak somehow. If we can't fix something, it must mean there is something wrong with us. Yet, when things aren't fixable, being with them is often the place of most peace and strength. While pain is an inevitable part of life, we don't need to add suffering to it through resisting and fighting against it. As therapists, this is a lesson we must learn both for ourselves and for our clients.

In the rest of this book, we'll examine how the practice of mindfulness meditation can help us develop the capacity to be with difficult things in the present moment, to understand the ways in which the mind attempts to draw us away, and to find the wellsprings of depth and presence in a multitasking world. Mindfulness, in other words, helps us cultivate the ability to simply be.

Note

1. All case examples are composites of experiences from my clinical practice. They do not refer to specific clients. All client names are fictitious.

2

WHAT IS MINDFULNESS?

A Taste of Mindfulness

In order to get a picture of what mindfulness entails, let's begin with some direct experience. Throughout the book, I'll be suggesting exercises for you to try. For some of the more involved exercises, I will describe them in the text and also provide a soundtrack to guide you through them. (See the Resources page at the end of the book for instructions on how to download the soundtracks.) I really encourage you to take the time to do the exercises, using either the written instructions or the soundtrack. Understanding mindfulness can't happen solely on an intellectual level. Just as you can't learn to swim by only reading books about the mechanics of swimming, you must experience mindfulness in order to begin to understand what it is all about. Some of the exercises will be challenging. There is a delicate balance here. I encourage you to try to stick it out through the challenging parts while also keeping in mind that mindfulness is not about hurting yourself or causing yourself undue suffering. If an exercise is too intense or uncomfortable, stop. Open your eyes. Take a walk. Play with the dog. You might want to try coming back to that exercise later, but nothing is gained by forcing yourself to do something that is harmful.

Our first exercise in mindfulness will be to bring mindful attention to a regular activity of daily life, an activity that many of us often do while our attention is directed elsewhere.

Exercise—A Taste of Mindfulness: Eating a Grape

- Begin by picking one grape from the bunch. As you do, notice the feel of the bunch of grapes as you select and pick one of them. Notice the sensation of pulling the grape away from its stem.
- **TOUCH** Using your sense of touch, explore the grape. Notice its texture, its weight, and whatever sensations arise as you roll it in your hand. If you feel comfortable doing so, notice how it feels against your cheek, the back of your hand, your forehead, or other parts of

---

the body. Take plenty of time to explore the grape with the sense of touch. As best you can, try to simply feel whatever sensations are there without labeling them in your mind.

- **SIGHT** Now, using your eyes, explore the grape in as much detail as you can. Look at the color of the grape. Is it all one color? What different colors are present? Look at the highlights and shadows, noticing how they transition one into the other and change as the grape rolls in your hand. Notice the shape of the grape. Notice whatever you can by using your sense of sight.
- **SMELL** See if there is any smell associated with the grape. As you hold the grape up to your nose, notice if there are any sensations in your mouth at the same time. Notice what thoughts you might be having.
- **MOVING** Now take the grape and move it to your mouth. As you do so, notice the sensations of movement in your arm and hand. Moving your arm slowly and deliberately may help in noticing. Notice the sensation in your fingers, the changing sensations in your arm as it moves. Rest the grape against your lips without putting it in your mouth just yet. Notice the sensations as you move it across your lips.
- **TASTE** Place the grape in your mouth but don't take a bite. Let it rest in your mouth and experience the sensations that arise as it does. Move it across your tongue, your cheek, the roof of your mouth. Notice both the grape and the sensations of movement.

Now, take just one bite of the grape. Notice whatever occurs. You might pay attention to taste, to texture, even to the sound of biting into the grape. Notice salivation. And notice how your mind reacts as you take only one bite.

Thoughtfully, chew the grape. Slow this process down more than you usually would. Notice how the flavor and texture change, if they do, as you chew. Notice how the tongue, teeth, and jaw work together in the chewing movement.

Now swallow the grape. Again, notice the physical sensations of swallowing. Is swallowing an event or a process? Notice when you know the grape has been swallowed.

- **REFLECTING** After you have swallowed the grape, sit quietly for a moment, reflecting on your experience. What was it like to bring your complete attention to eating one grape? What did you learn about eating and grapes and the reactions of your mind in the process? While it may seem odd to take this much time to eat a grape, imagine what it would be like to bring this same level of awareness to hugging your child, to talking with your partner, to listening to your client, to watching a lingering sunset, to making love.

The Path to Being

The exercise of eating a grape while bringing full attention to the process is really an experiment in mindfulness, and a venture into the being mode of mind. In the rest of the chapter, we'll explore in depth the components of mindfulness, what the practice of mindfulness can teach us about how our minds operate, and how we can then develop the capacity to become aware of and change our mode of mind to better suit whatever circumstances in which we might find ourselves. But we will start by considering some of the misconceptions about mindfulness that many of us have, based on societal views of meditation and contemplative practices.

Misconceptions

Beginning to understand mindfulness requires that we question some of our beliefs about what mindfulness practice is and what states of mind it results in. We have lots of societal images of meditation.[1] I've included one here.

Figure 2.1
Copyright: Yellowj/Shutterstock.com

It looks lovely doesn't it? Who wouldn't want to be in such a state . . . beautiful, young, flexible, serene, with a flat stomach and gorgeous hair, enjoying a peaceful, natural landscape? The problem is that mindfulness practice may not help us achieve any of those things. Nor do we have to already possess any of these qualities in order to benefit from mindfulness practice. How meditation is typically portrayed in the media and advertising has very little to do with the actual experience of meditating. However, we carry those images with us as we begin to try our hand at meditation. When we don't seem to be getting the same results as the woman in the picture (and we never do), we decide that something is wrong. We may decide that meditation is for the birds and doesn't really work. Or we become convinced that we have failed at meditating and are somehow deficient. In either case, the understandable temptation is to stop doing something that isn't living up to our expectations. The real answer, however, is to examine our expectations. One way to do that is to look at what mindfulness practice *isn't* about.

We most often think of meditation or mindfulness as producing a state of physical and emotional relaxation. I used to have a colleague who always greeted me upon my return from meditation retreats with the statement, "Wow, you must be so mellow!" Often, it wasn't the case. The process of getting to know your mind in the moment can be relaxing, of course, but it can also be difficult, boring, or filled with strong emotion as you will discover when you try it. When your meditation practice doesn't provide you with relaxation or make you physically and emotionally serene like the woman in the picture above appears to be, it doesn't mean that you, or the practice, have failed. Mindfulness is about learning to be present with whatever is going on at any given moment, not about trying to change your experience, or achieving a particular state of being. For instance, if you feel sleepy while doing your mindfulness practice, and are able to be present with that sleepiness, you're doing it right. If you feel sleepy and aren't able to be present but come to realize you aren't present and bring your attention back to the sleepy feelings, you're also doing it right. Realizing you weren't present is a moment of waking up to what's really going on for you. Finally, feeling sleepy while meditating and deciding to get up and take a nap is also doing it right! In addition to being aware of what is happening in the moment, mindfulness practice also asks us to be compassionate with ourselves. Sometimes that means stopping the formal practice of mindfulness to take care of ourselves in other ways. There is plenty of suffering in our lives without adding another source and calling it mindfulness. It is the effort to cultivate a clear awareness of *whatever* we find in our experience that separates mindfulness practice from simple relaxation strategies.

Another vision of meditation is that it puts us in a trance or leaves us with an empty mind as thoughts subside. While this may be a goal for some types of meditation practice, thoughts are not seen as undesirable in the mindfulness world. In fact, understanding how thoughts arise, when they can be useful tools, and when it may be better not to take them so literally, are some of the primary benefits of mindfulness practice. If anything, mindfulness brings us more in touch with our mind and how it works. As for going into a trance, I hope your experience with eating the grape showed you that mindfulness is about being keenly connected to what you are doing and experiencing, and is not designed to numb or deaden your awareness. Mindfulness is about showing up for your life, not trying to avoid it.

Finally, we often think of meditation as a technique, a quick fix to apply when we're feeling stressed or anxious. In fact, mindfulness practice is a lifelong pursuit and one not restricted to the meditation cushion. In this way, mindfulness practice is more like a vitamin tablet than an aspirin. Taking a vitamin when you are seeking immediate relief from a headache doesn't make much sense. Vitamins help us build a foundation of health and capacity that may allow us to deal with life's difficulties more competently and may ultimately keep us from getting a headache. But once we have a headache, vitamins don't provide much immediate relief. In my experience, mindfulness works much the same way. Can mindfulness help us deal better with pain, anxiety, depression, and other difficult states of mind and being? Yes, but it does so best in the context of regular practice. Regular practice helps to build fundamental capacity—more focused attention, greater awareness of our bodies, less distraction by thoughts and feelings that aren't useful at the time, and so forth. Sporadic practice or practicing only when we want to relax or change something that is upsetting will prove ultimately unsatisfying. Despite the fact that we're bombarded by media promises of quick-fix solutions—"Ten ways to save your marriage," "Two simple exercises that will give you a trim waistline forever"—most of what we struggle with in life isn't amenable to a quick fix. As one of my friends noted, if quick-fix self-help books are effective, why do so many of them keep coming out month after month? But that's the good news for mindfulness practice. It provides us a way to ground ourselves in awareness and experience that can last a lifetime and that will gradually ease the obstacles that get in the way of living a rich and fulfilling life. As therapists, it helps us step into the being mode with our clients and provide them an experience of depth and presence they rarely find elsewhere.

Mindlessness

One of my clients told me recently, "You know, it isn't that hard to have an out-of-body experience." He was talking about the amount of time we spend only vaguely aware of where we are, what's happening around us, and what our inner experience is. For almost all of us, this is a typical experience and a state of mind we might call *mindlessness*. Mindlessness manifests itself in our daily lives in a variety of ways. Brown and Ryan (2003, p. 826) give the following examples of mindlessness:

- "I break or spill things because of carelessness, not paying attention, or thinking of something else."
- "I tend not to notice feelings of physical tension or discomfort until they really grab my attention."
- "I find myself listening to someone with one ear, doing something else at the same time."
- "I tend to walk quickly to get where I'm going without paying attention to what I experience along the way."

I suspect these examples are familiar to most of us.

When immersed in mindlessness, we are operating on automatic pilot. We've all had the experience of knowing we got in our car at home and ending up at our intended destination but not having any recollection of the actual journey, especially if it is a familiar route. Like an airliner flying on autopilot with little or no attention from the crew, we have navigated our way successfully but with little awareness. But where were we during the trip? As my client noticed, the mind leaves the body, and the present moment, for a variety of destinations. We spend a lot of time lost in fantasies, extending our thoughts into the future to either fear or anticipate what might happen in our lives, or reliving moments of the past with enjoyment or regret. As a daily commuter in the Washington, DC area, I spend a fair amount of time in my car. One of the things I've noticed during those daily trips is that I spend a lot of that time rehearsing for things I think will happen. I might be concerned about a difficult conversation I need to have with a student or a colleague at work. I might anticipate what I want to talk about with the dear old friend with whom I have a lunch date. Sometimes it extends into my clinical work as I work out what to say to a client whose work with me seems stalled. And it isn't always a conversation that I find myself rehearsing. I might think about the route of the walk I'll take with the dog when I get home. Since this is the way most of us spend most of our time, it seems hardly worth remarking on. As my mindfulness practice grew, however, I began to realize that almost all of the time, I was rehearsing for things *that never actually occurred*. The colleague with whom I needed to have a hard talk wasn't at work that day. It was raining when I got home and the dog had to be satisfied with a quick trip around the backyard. Lunch began with my friend sharing bad news that took our attention. And the client came to her appointment talking about a resounding new realization she had had since our last session. I had rehearsed for each encounter but each time found myself in an unexpected play.

Since it seems so ubiquitous, it is hard to believe there is much of a problem with mindlessness. Isn't it, at worst, a harmless waste of time? Let's examine how it might affect our work as therapists. Imagine, for a moment, that you are about to see one of your current challenging clients. I'll tell you about one of mine. Alec came to see me after his wife of 12 years told him it was either therapy or divorce as far as she was concerned. Alec appeared in my office equally shaken by his wife's ultimatum and utterly confused by it. At first blush, Alec had a lot of things going for him. He was an up-and-coming partner in a local high-tech firm that had had good success in winning subcontracts from larger companies. His technical expertise was well respected both in his own company and among their competitors, where he was seen as something of a visionary when it came to spotting developing trends in his industry. He and his wife had a 7-year-old daughter for whom he cared deeply, and the family had money enough to travel regularly and live comfortably. So, what brought Alec to therapy?

"Eileen—my wife—says I'm not really there," he told me at our first meeting. "I don't have a clue what she's talking about."

Alec paused and I began to ask him to clarify what his wife actually said to him, but then he continued, talking over my first few words. He looked out the large window in my office, turning his face away from me.

"I'm home every night. I don't run around on her. She should hear some of the things that go on with the other partners."

Once again, I was ready to say something but Alec interrupted me.

"No, no," he said. "I have to get this out."

He turned back to the window, speaking now as if I were only a bystander to his soliloquy.

"I knew it was going to turn out this way. I knew it wasn't going to work out. God, I'm such an idiot . . ."

As the session continued, I began to get a good sense of what Alec's wife found so difficult about him. Most of my attempts to connect with him in that first session were shuffled aside as Alec continued to talk. But it didn't feel like he was telling *me* his story, the person sitting only a few feet from him, trying my best to understand. I gradually felt myself getting irritated with Alec as he kept me at arm's length. Finally, I stopped him in mid-sentence. He turned from the window to look at me.

"I know," he said. "You want me to stop. I get that all the time. But I'm just afraid that if I don't say what I have on my mind, I'll lose it." And he began to talk again, my effort to begin a real conversation with him apparently ignored.

Alec was a challenging client for me. His emotional wariness and ability to keep me at arm's distance, to keep his real experience of himself and his life hidden, from himself as well as from me, left me frustrated, angered, and discouraged in turn. While clearly wanting my help, he seemed unable or unwilling to give me the openings I need to provide it. And the less I was able to bring mindfulness to these encounters, the more likely I was to respond reactively to Alec, responses that only furthered the distance between us.

Submerged in a mind*less* state, one temptation is to slip into judgment. It can go both ways. At times, I felt Alec was keeping me so far away on purpose, in an effort to frustrate me. "What a controlling jerk," I found myself thinking. "He must have some kind of character disorder." At other times, I turned the judgment on myself. "You must be losing your touch. A guy like this would never have been a problem before. Maybe all this mindfulness stuff is making you soft. You'd have been right in there confronting him a few years ago." Neither stance was very helpful in dealing thoughtfully with Alec.

At other times, I found myself rehearsing sessions with Alec in my mind long before I was scheduled to see him again. I'd play out things I'd like to tell him, questions I'd like the answer to. It was more than a simple dialog in my mind, however. There was a visceral, tense feeling to these internal conversations, as if Alec had somehow crawled inside me, and the tension I felt with him in session had now taken over my body. Part of the problem with these imagined conversations was that they began to coalesce into a picture of Alec that was only partially accurate. The next time I saw him, it was as though I was taking my internal and imagined interactions into the session with me. The conversations I had practiced in my head began to seem like a treatment plan—"I'll say this, and then I'll say that." It was hard to let go of that imagined conversation and simply be present with Alec, responding to what he was actually saying rather than to the internal image I had of him. On a more subtle level, those imagined interactions with Alec—especially if they added to my frustration or irritation with him—would emotionally color our actual interaction. I ran the risk of reacting less to Alec as he *actually was* in that moment and more to who I *imagined* him to be. The more entrenched we become in our imagined views of situations and people, the more they color what we perceive about the world—becoming self-fulfilling prophecies. Without a perspective grounded in mindfulness, my imagined sense could seem more real than what I might be experiencing were I more present. Mindfulness, then, offers us an antidote to mindlessness and its threat that a preoccupation with our inner narratives and rehearsals begins to seem more real than the actual experiences around us. A mindful stance can help us correct our imagined views and be present with what is actually before us.

14

So What Is Mindfulness?

Now that we have some idea of what mindfulness isn't, let's see if we can get an idea of what mindfulness actually is. I want to begin with a caution. We can certainly use language to describe mindfulness, and it can be very helpful to have a cognitive understanding of it, but mindfulness must be experienced to be truly known. To that end, I'll suggest some brief exercises throughout the rest of the chapter to help you experience the components of mindfulness. I know it is hard to interrupt the flow of reading to participate in an exercise, but I encourage you to do so. Mindfulness is about getting both our real and metaphorical hands dirty in the world of our experience. Failure to do so leaves us with only the barest hint of what mindfulness can deliver.

Stepping Into the Moment

As my client noted, we spend a majority of our time out of our bodies, and out of the present moment. Therefore, the first component of mindfulness is making an intentional decision to step out of whatever story line or daydream we might be involved in. It represents our intention to show up for our current life and experience, to be present. We already have some common wisdom tools for this. How many times have you told yourself to just take a deep breath when you found yourself about to react to a situation in a way that you knew would not be to your, or anyone else's, benefit? I've done that plenty of times. A deep breath can be a good way to step into the moment because it grounds us in the body—a good doorway into the present. Coming into the present moment also means stepping out of autopilot mode. Meditation teacher and therapist Tara Brach calls this process "the sacred pause." It is a wonderful and useful description. Pausing is like taking a break, allowing ourselves a step back from whatever activity we've been engaged in. When we ate the grape mindfully, the first step was to pause—to drop whatever other physical and mental activity we were engaged in and bring our five senses to bear on the grape. What does stepping into the moment look like in everyday life? You can do it nearly anywhere.

One of my favorite places to step into the moment is in line at the grocery store. I can usually feel myself start to grow tense and impatient if I have to wait more than a few moments to check out. There always seem to be a dozen more useful things to do than stand in line. My impatience often shows up as judgment. It's easy to become critical of the clerk who "should" be doing her job faster or the next customer who "should" be getting his credit card out of his wallet now instead of waiting until all his items are rung up. In this situation, stepping into the moment begins with a conscious intention to interrupt the cycle of impatience and criticism.

I first bring my attention to my body. It helps me to notice the sensations of standing—the pressure of my feet on the floor, the slight sway of my body as I stand, the temperature of the air against my skin. I might also notice how irritation is affecting me—the vague pressure at my temples, my tight grip on my grocery list. I try to notice my breathing for a moment, feeling the physical sensations of exhaling and inhaling and looking for the place of calm that I know, from my more formal meditation practice, is in the breath. Grounding in the body allows me to create some distance from my agitated thoughts and loosens their hold.

Stepping into the moment can be as simple or as elaborate as you need it to be. Sometimes it is as simple as taking a moment to reconnect with the body while in line at the store. It may also mean realizing that you are struggling to stay present with a client and bringing your attention to the breath to center yourself. Or it may mean making the preparations to attend a week-long silent meditation retreat—a much more elaborate step out of business as usual. Whatever form it takes, mindfulness begins with *an intention to be present*.

Exercise

Experiment with stepping into the present moment. When you notice that you are elsewhere—lost in thoughts, daydreaming, irritated, or edgy—renew your intention to be present. Bring your attention to whatever physical sensations present themselves. You can do this in a whole host of situations. Try stepping into the present moment just before you begin client sessions, and any time you find yourself distracted in therapy. Remember, you are developing your intention to be present.

Focus

Once we have intentionally stepped into the present moment, we use an anchor to help us keep our attention there. The traditional anchor for mindfulness meditation practice is the breath, the physical sensations of breathing. The breath is a useful anchor for a number of reasons. First, it is always available. If you aren't breathing, you need something other than meditation! In addition to being available, it is generally unobtrusive. I can pay attention to my breathing in many situations without drawing undue attention to myself or disturbing those around me. I could also use chanting as an anchor, for instance, but I can only imagine the looks I'd get if I suddenly began chanting while waiting for my groceries to be rung up. The breath is also very responsive to our general emotional state; noticing how you are breathing can help you recognize your overall mood state. When I am anxious, my breath becomes shallow and rapid and centered high in my chest, right behind my breastbone. As I relax, my breath slows and becomes centered in my lower abdomen. Finally, the breath can be either voluntary or involuntary—that is, breathing can either happen on its own without our guidance or we can make ourselves breathe in a certain manner, including not breathing at all for a time by holding our breath. The dual nature of the breath gives us a good laboratory for learning to let our experience happen without forcing it. The initial instruction in breath-centered meditation is simply to observe the sensations of breathing as they arise on their own. This proves more difficult than it sounds. However, as we are become more adept at simply observing the breath, we can then bring this noninterfering attention to other aspects of our experience such as other body sensations, or thoughts, or emotions. There is no more fundamental experience of the doing mode (breathing intentionally) and the being mode (letting the breath come as it will, without interfering).

While the breath is the traditional anchor for mindfulness practice, there are many other possible anchors as well. The body scan—in which careful attention is directed to each part of the body in turn, experiencing whatever sensations are present—is another traditional meditation practice, for instance. While attention to body sensations is traditional and useful for many people, be aware that not everyone finds comfort in the body or in paying attention to it. Attending to feelings in the body can be tremendously upsetting for some people who have a history of abuse or trauma, particularly sexual abuse, or who have intensely negative feelings about their body. Paying attention to body sensations can create a sense of disgust or a smothering sense of entrapment in the body. In these cases, using another anchor is the best course of action; attending to sounds in the environment is an anchor that can create a sense of spaciousness and distance that feels safe.

Some meditation traditions use a simple phrase or *mantra* that is repeated silently to oneself to anchor attention. This phrase may be meaningful ("May I feel peace"), it may have a sound that is symbolic (the mantra "Om" is said to be the primordial sound from which the universe and all within it arose), or it may be a simple sound or syllable with no particular meaning. Later in the book, we will examine *metta* or lovingkindness meditation in which a set of statements designed to cultivate compassion and lovingkindness are used as the anchor. Regardless of what it is, mindfulness practice asks us to focus on an anchor to help us bring our attention to the present moment. As we become more skillful at doing so, we become better able to see our experience clearly and understand what the meditation teacher and therapist Sylvia Boorstein calls our habits of mind.

Distraction

While bringing attention to the breath sounds like a simple enterprise, it quickly becomes clear that our minds distract us almost immediately when we try to do so. In one instant we are paying close attention to the sensations of breathing, and in the next, we are planning what to have for dinner, recalling an old romance from high school, or wondering what the high point of our next vacation will be. An unexplained noise outside the room where we are meditating can quickly lead to an elaborate fantasy about what might have caused it. If we manage to maintain our focus through this, physical sensations may arise that are a distraction—sleepiness or agitation or pain. Everything about us, it seems, is intent on taking our attention away from the breath.

Recognition

The mind's distraction from the present can last for a few seconds, or for hours, weeks, or even months. In the short term, the mind distracts us from the anchor we have chosen to focus on, we quickly recognize that we are lost in thought, and bring our attention back to the anchor. At other times, however, the mind convinces us that we need to stop meditating immediately to take care of some task we mistakenly left undone. The idea is accompanied by a strong sense of urgency and agitation and suddenly we are off doing the dishes instead of meditating. It may not be until the next day that we realize we have been lost in a world of thoughts and stories and rehearsals and doing and now it is time to come back to the meditation cushion and back to our efforts to simply be in the present moment. At other times, we become lost in a story of frustration and hopelessness about our meditation practice and stop meditating for months. The time frame may differ but the process is the same.

It is tempting to lapse into judgment and self-blame when we realize that we are not focused on the present, that we have lost track of the breath, and are having a mental argument with our fourth-grade teacher who we always felt mistreated us. After all, losing track of the breath must mean we aren't doing it right, that we're failures at meditating and will never gain anything from it. We quickly conjure up visions of other meditators who never waver in their focus and dedication. But calling ourselves failures isn't accurate. Distraction is simply a natural part of the process of what minds do. However, we also have the capacity to recognize when we are no longer focused on the breath. This capacity—the ability to "wake up" from an immersion in the stories and narratives and distractions of the mind—is what we intend to develop in mindfulness practice. Every time we recognize that we are distracted, we strengthen the capacity to bring intentional focus to our experience.

Return

After recognizing that our attention is elsewhere, we do our best to bring the mind back from wherever it has taken us and refocus on the breath. This act demands kindness, not force. If we recognize that wandering away from the anchor is simply the mind at work—the mind trying to return to the familiarity of the doing mode—we can treat ourselves with kindness as we bring the mind back. My cat J.J. taught me the importance of kindness and allowing a number of years ago. J.J. was fascinated by my meditation practice. No sooner would I spread out my mat and sit down on my bench than he would come to investigate. Investigation involved walking back and forth on the little strip of exposed mat in front of me, rubbing his head against my knees and hands as I sat. I did my best to ignore him, but if I didn't reach out to scratch his ears, he became more insistent. My first efforts to handle the situation were to shoo J.J. away. If you have a cat, you know how unsuccessful that effort was. The more I tried to get J.J. to do what I wanted, the more insistent he became on parading back and forth in front of me. Next I tried keeping him beside me, hoping he would lie quietly while I meditated. No luck here, either. One day, rather than struggle with him, I simply picked him up and held him cradled in my arms—no pressure, no effort to keep him near or make him go away. Somewhat to my surprise, he settled down quickly and lay purring as I began my practice for the day. After a few minutes, he grew tired of being held, wriggled out of my arms, and left me undisturbed for the rest of my meditation. It became a familiar game over the following weeks. J.J. would stop by to be held for a few minutes before either wandering off or settling in next to me quietly on my meditation mat. Using the same attitude of gentle holding and kindness that I used with J.J., rather than forcing, can also be very useful when dealing with the wandering mind. So bring your mind back gently and do your best not to force it to stay on the breath. Embrace it gently, and when it wanders, be patient.

It is easy to describe the components of mindfulness practice in words. The cycle seems straightforward—Intention to be present, Focus, Distraction, Recognition, and Return. Practice is a different matter. Doing mode is familiar territory and it occurs not just in physical action but also in the activity of the mind itself. Hanson and Mendius (2009) suggest that the evolutionary survival functions of the brain must be overcome in order to quiet the mind. The brain evolved to constantly scan the environment for danger, usually manifested as something changing unexpectedly. Active minds, in other words, had a survival advantage. Unfortunately, the web of relationships we live in—physical environment, social environment, emotional environment—is always changing. While many of those changes don't indicate danger the way a movement in the bushes that might be a leopard did, the evolutionary history of the brain keeps it activated. In addition to scanning the environment, the brain is also excellent at constructing models of what could happen, helping prepare us to avoid danger by imagining the outcomes of various courses of action. Reliving past experiences also helps by letting us imagine alternatives in situations that didn't go as well as we might like. These are the many rehearsals that I described above. You can certainly feel the power of those deep evolutionary lessons when you sit down with your eyes closed and your back straight, and try to keep your focus on your breath. The mind tries desperately at times to not give up its active, doing-oriented, protective role. I hope this helps you be patient with yourself and your experience because there is much to be gained. Zindel Segal describes the promise of mindfulness as follows:

> At the heart of mindfulness lies, not a desire to suppress this inner restlessness, but a nonjudgmental curiosity about it, and a willingness to simply observe it as it happens. Making friends with our attention—not beating it (and ourselves) up when it drifts from its intended focus—helps teach us how to deal with other deviations from perfection in ourselves and others. When we're berating ourselves for falling short of our own expectations, mindfulness practice teaches us to bring the same type of gentle awareness to these self-denigrating thoughts and feelings in our everyday lives.
>
> (Segal, 2008, p. 1)

As therapists, mindfulness practice teaches us not just to do something. It teaches us to be.

Note

1. This is a book primarily about mindfulness meditation or mindfulness practice. I will use the term *meditation* to indicate the larger category of contemplative practices, of which mindfulness is one.

3

WHAT DO WE KNOW ABOUT MINDFULNESS?

The Research Record

Before we look at the specific ways in which mindfulness can benefit therapists, I want to briefly review the research literature on the benefits of mindfulness in general. The research literature on mindfulness is growing dramatically and I plan to review only the highlights because new mindfulness applications are constantly being tested and new findings published. The pace is such that any review will likely soon be out of date.

General Effects of Mindfulness

Mindfulness has been associated with a variety of positive outcomes. Sedlmeier et al. (2012) performed a meta-analysis of research studies on meditation. A meta-analysis is a technique for combining research findings across many studies to examine outcomes in a larger context. In their meta-analysis, Sedlmeier et al. looked at studies that investigated mindfulness in nonclinical adult populations. They found 595 studies that were eligible for the analysis—evidence for the tremendous interest in mindfulness in the scientific community—but only 163 of these studies were scientifically sound enough to merit final inclusion. The studies examined a broad range of mindfulness practices, including things like transcendental meditation and yoga, which do result in mindful states. They also looked at a wide range of outcomes including such things as anxiety, interpersonal relationships, negative emotions, self-concept, stress, well-being, concentration, attention, and so forth. Looking across all studies and all outcomes combined, the findings of this study indicate that meditation has a measurable and at least a moderate positive effect. When looking at specific outcomes, the effects varied as we might expect. Interestingly, the strongest effect was found in the realm of interpersonal relationships. The studies in this areas measured things like relationship satisfaction, relationship distress, closeness, and feelings of relatedness. The meta-analysis found a strong positive effect across these studies. The next strongest outcomes were found in the area of negative emotions, indicating that meditation helped attenuate things like anxiety, anger, worry, confusion, tension, and guilt. While this study also raised a number of issues that need to be dealt with in future research on the impact of meditation and mindfulness, it is clear that these practices have general benefits for nonclinical populations.

We can also point to a number of specific benefits from mindfulness meditation in the general population. Chambers, Lo, and Allen (2007) studied 20 novice meditators who participated in an intensive 10-day mindfulness meditation retreat. Not surprisingly, those participants who completed the retreat reported higher levels of mindfulness than those in the control group. In addition, the retreat participants reported significant decreases in ruminative thinking and depressive symptoms and enhancement of working memory and sustained attention. Working memory is kind of like our mental scratch pad that helps us stay on track with tasks in the face of distractions. It also helps regulate emotion. Other studies have shown that mindfulness helps strengthen working memory in nonclinical groups. Jha, Stanley, Kiyonaga, Wong, and Gelfand (2010) studied the impact of mindfulness training on members of the military who were being deployed to a combat zone. Those who did not get the mindfulness intervention saw decreases in working memory capacity over the course of their clearly stressful deployment. Among those who got the mindfulness intervention, amount of meditation practice was related to the strength of the effect. Those who practiced less saw decreases in working memory capacity while those who practiced more actually saw increases despite the stress of the deployment. Practice time was also associated with affect regulation, with those who practiced more having lower negative and higher positive affect. The authors go on to suggest that mindfulness practice may be a way to protect individuals in stressful situations from the decreases in functioning that are often seen. Mindfulness can also help improve our ability to focus. Moore and Malinowski (2009) compared experienced mindfulness meditators with a nonmeditating control group on measures of attention and cognitive flexibility. The authors define cognitive flexibility as "the human ability to adapt cognitive processing strategies to face new and unexpected conditions" (p. 177). The findings from this study suggest that mindfulness is positively related to both better attention performance and increased cognitive flexibility.

Ortner, Kilner, and Zelazo (2007) examined the effect of mindfulness meditation on emotional reactivity in two related studies. In the first study, they found that more experienced meditators were better able to perform a cognitive task after viewing upsetting pictures than less experienced meditators. In the second study, they trained participants with no meditation experience in mindfulness and again examined the interference of upsetting pictures on performing a cognitive task. Those who were trained in meditation did better on the cognitive task than those in the control group who did not receive meditation training, suggesting that mindfulness helps practitioners disengage more quickly from emotionally charged experiences.

Finally, as reported in the Hofmann and Sawyer (2010) meta-analysis, mindfulness appears to improve relationship satisfaction. In two related studies, Barnes, Brown, Krusemark, Campbell, and Rogge (2007) looked at levels of trait mindfulness and relationship satisfaction among dating college couples. In the second study, they measured partners' mindfulness and then asked the couple to participate in a stressful conversation, after which a number of relationship factors were measured. Mindfulness was positively correlated with overall relationship satisfaction. After the difficult discussion exercise, those with higher mindfulness scores had lower levels of emotional stress including less anxiety and less hostility. Further exploration suggests that this finding occurred because those with higher mindfulness scores *enter* difficult situations with lower levels of anxiety and hostility. Trait mindfulness was also associated with less negative relationship evaluation after the difficult discussion exercise. Finally, there were some positive effects of trait mindfulness on behaviorally observed communication among the couples.

Wachs and Cordova (2007) looked at the association between mindfulness and marital quality with a focus on specific emotional skills with which mindfulness might be associated. Mindfulness appears to be associated with partners' ability to identify and effectively communicate their emotions as well as regulate their expression of anger. These skills seem to be the pathway by which mindfulness is then associated with marital satisfaction and quality.

Chiesa and Serretti (2009) looked specifically at the effects of Mindfulness-Based Stress Reduction—an 8-week mindfulness-based program—on healthy people. I'll describe MBSR in more detail later since it is primarily aimed at people struggling with specific disorders. In a so-called healthy population, MBSR is primarily used for stress reduction. Chiesa and Serretti found only 10 studies that looked at MBSR in this population. However, they were able to aggregate the data and calculate effect sizes. MBSR had a number of positive effects. As one would expect from a stress reduction program, MBSR did reduce stress compared to no treatment, and it also appeared to do so in one study compared to a placebo condition that had the same amount of group time and instructor attention but did not teach mindfulness. In addition to stress reduction, MBSR also increased scores on a measure of spirituality and decreased ruminative thinking. While relaxation training also reduced rumination, MBSR performed significantly better in this regard. The mindful approach to disturbing thoughts—that is, observing them nonjudgmentally without becoming entangled in them—certainly seems to help with rumination. Finally, MBSR produced increases in empathy and self-compassion, both of which could help improve relationship satisfaction.

Among nonclinical groups, then, we see that mindfulness is associated with better attention control, more cognitive flexibility, better working memory, less emotional reactivity, and better relational functioning. While there are other specific ways in which mindfulness appears to help therapists, these fundamental skills would seem to serve therapists well, indeed.

Mindfulness for Physical and Psychological Problems

While the evidence we've just reviewed suggests that mindfulness can help people who are not seeking help for clinical problems, much more research exists about the application of mindfulness and mindfulness-based therapies to physical and psychological health problems. Mindfulness approaches have been used with a broad range of presenting problems, including anxiety, depression, chronic pain, eating disorders, the effects of cancer treatment, and so on. Mindfulness is incorporated into medical and psychological treatments in a variety of ways. Some treatments are largely based on mindfulness practice. Mindfulness-Based Stress Reduction (MBSR; Kabat-Zinn, 1990) is an example of one such program. MBSR was developed in the late 1970s at the University of Massachusetts Medical Center by Jon Kabat-Zinn, who believed, from his own experience as a student of Zen, *vipassana,* and yoga, that meditation and mindfulness practice could be helpful to patients to whom traditional medicine seemed to offer little hope. Kabat-Zinn found that *vipassana,* or insight meditation (the basis for the practices I am describing in this book), was a good vehicle to bring mindfulness practice into mainstream Western medicine because it did not rely on ritual, explicit Buddhist philosophy, or on a strong student-teacher relationship. It could be taught, in other words, as a secular practice. MBSR uses basic Buddhist meditation practices as a foundation including mindful movement through gentle yoga, body awareness through the body scan meditation, and sitting meditation with an emphasis on breath focus to cultivate concentration followed by widening consciousness to investigate the arising and passing of all experience. The formal MBSR program is 8 weeks in length including a day-long silent retreat experience. The primary content of this program is designed to cultivate the development of mindful awareness, and participants are explicitly taught to meditate in a classical way as the primary intervention.

MBSR has been applied to a wide range of physical and psychological issues and populations. It has been used with depression and the prevention of relapse following major depression, anxiety, substance abuse, eating disorders, insomnia, chronic pain, psoriasis, type 2 diabetes, rheumatoid arthritis, ADD/ADHS, and cancer (see Cullen, 2011, and Praissman, 2008, for reviews of the MBSR literature). MBSR has also spawned variations aimed at specific disorders, such as Mindfulness-Based Cognitive Therapy (Segal, Williams, & Teasdale, 2002), which has been demonstrated to reduce relapse following episodes of major depression.

Other therapy approaches are not based primarily on mindfulness practices but integrate or include them as part of the treatment model. Hayes, Strosahl, and Wilson (2011), for instance, developed an approach to therapy that relies on cognitive-behavioral models but integrates acceptance and mindfulness practices. Acceptance and commitment therapy (ACT) has a number of parallels to Buddhist psychology (see Hayes, 2003), but formal mindfulness meditation is not necessarily taught as part of the treatment. In addition, the model relies on a number of other components that are not part of formal mindfulness practice, such as planning and taking committed action based on one's espoused life values. Dialectical behavior therapy (DBT; Linehan, 1993) makes use of mindfulness skills in the treatment of borderline personality disorder, but, like ACT, relies on a number of other components from the cognitive-behavioral therapies.

Finally, mindfulness can be incorporated into therapy through the therapist's own practice of it. This approach posits that mindfulness practices help the therapist develop stronger therapeutic presence, more equanimity in the face of difficult material, and greater personal resilience (McCollum & Gehart, 2010). The next chapter will explore this way of integrating mindfulness into therapy.

Outcome Research in Health Care/Psychological Arenas

Compared to research on nonclinical populations, there is a large and robust body of research on people experiencing mindfulness-based intervention to deal with physical or psychological problems. Baer (2003) conducted an early review of the literature on the effectiveness of mindfulness for a variety of psychological and physical conditions and found mindfulness useful for a variety of problems. Chronic pain patients manifest significant improvement in pain, improvement in other physical symptoms, and improvement in psychological functioning as well. These outcomes were maintained at follow-up. Baer also concluded that anxiety and panic disorders profited from mindfulness treatment, with decreases in symptoms being maintained, in one study, up to 3 years. There is also a strong body of evidence to support the use of mindfulness as a primary intervention with some cognitive components to help prevent relapse following major depression (Segal et al., 2002). In the realm of physical health, Baer reports studies that show improvements in a variety of symptoms when fibromyalgia patients are taught mindfulness.

Kabat-Zinn and colleagues found that listening to mindfulness tapes during light treatment for psoriasis reduced treatment times significantly while reducing psychological distress as well (Kabat-Zinn et al., 1998). Patients who received the mindfulness intervention had clear skin after a median of 65 days compared to 97 days for the group that received light therapy alone. Other studies found that MBSR decreased psychological distress and mood disturbance in cancer patients with gains being maintained at a 6-month follow-up. Baer reports 3 studies that used mixed clinical samples—that is, patients presenting for treatment with a variety of diagnoses. In each study, a mindfulness intervention produced positive changes in a variety of clinical measures.

In addition to reporting on clinical outcomes, Baer also found several studies that examined patients' reactions to the mindfulness intervention they experienced. The studies found generally high rates of satisfaction and high ratings of the importance of the mindfulness interventions among patients who had completed treatment. This finding bears cautious interpretation, of course. Had patients who dropped out of treatment been included, the ratings might be have been lower. However, treatments that patients are satisfied with may be better tolerated and complied with than those that patients do not find as useful. Baer's assessment of the literature in 2003 was that most of the studies lacked methodological rigor and that well-designed studies were needed to advance our understanding of the effects of mindfulness for clinical problems.

Since Baer's early review, the research literature on mindfulness has grown substantially. Khoury et al. (2013) conducted a meta-analysis of the mindfulness literature and, in their initial survey, they found more than 2,800 citations for mindfulness. Selecting only the most rigorous studies reduced the total number to 209. However, more than 12,000 participants were involved in these studies—a large subject pool. The problem areas studies ranged widely in the studies, with anxiety and cancer being the most common, followed by pain, substance abuse, fibromyalgia, obesity, HIV, PTSD, and headache. Also represented were ADHD, psychosis, personality disorders, child sexual abuse, irritable bowel syndrome, brain injury, heart disease, tinnitus, multiple sclerosis, and rheumatoid arthritis. This list alone is instructive because of the wide range of disorders examined in these studies compared to the relatively small range of disorders Baer (2003) reported on.

Khoury et al. (2013) conclude that mindfulness-based therapies produce good outcomes when studied in pretest–posttest only designs, when compared to a no-treatment control group, and when compared to some other active treatments. Mindfulness-based therapies did not differ from traditional cognitive-behavioral treatments nor from pharmacological treatments. The studies found that mindfulness-based therapies were especially effective in reducing anxiety, depression, and stress.

Clearly we are accumulating a strong body of research supporting the use of mindfulness and mindfulness-based interventions for both physical and psychological problems. The amount of time and effort devoted to investigating mindfulness is significant and speaks to the confidence that clinicians and researchers have that mindfulness can produce good outcomes. Norcross, Pfund, and Prochaska (2013) conducted a survey of 70 psychotherapy experts and asked them what they believed the trends in psychotherapy would be over the next 30 years. The experts identified a variety of things that they believed would affect the future of psychotherapy, including a variety of electronic and Web-based innovations like the use of virtual reality and smartphone applications to provide services. They believe evidence-based practices will be increasingly required in various practice settings, and that breakthroughs in neuroscience will increasingly affect therapy. They also believe that the effectiveness of therapy will continue to increase and that therapeutic interventions will be increasingly tailored to specific client characteristics like culture, gender, and stage of change. While many of the predicted changes rely on technology and new scientific discoveries, the authors also note: "Ironically, unlike technology, the ideas that embody several of the highest rankings derive from ancient Eastern philosophies. Such modifications include mindfulness and meditation, as stand-alone theories or techniques, or integrated as part of dialectical behavior therapy and acceptance and commitment therapy" (p. 369). Specifically, the experts in the Norcross study believe that the theoretical orientation that will see the most increased use in the next 30 years will be mindfulness and mindfulness-based therapies.

4

HOW DOES MINDFULNESS BENEFIT THERAPISTS?

When I was first starting out as a young therapist, I worked at a mental health clinic in a medium-sized Midwestern city. Because our sliding scale fees were low, we saw clients from across all economic and social groups, some of whom were quite skeptical about therapy. I still remember one man who came to three court-ordered sessions after his girlfriend called the police while he was in the midst of an angry outburst—screaming and threatening to hit her. Sonny managed to patch it up with his girlfriend, who verified that this was an isolated incident, quite out of character for him. He was appropriately contrite about his verbal assault on her, recognized that his alcohol use that night had contributed to it, and finally agreed with me that a stress management group was probably the best bet for him. He agreed to seek one out and attend voluntarily.

Sonny was a roofer and came to his last session right from work in a sweaty T-shirt and tar-stained jeans. I could see a split thumbnail where he had apparently hit himself with a hammer. It was 92 degrees outside that summer afternoon and I couldn't imagine what the temperature was on a roof.

"Thanks a lot, doc," he said to me as we were winding up the session. "I think you really helped me see what was going on. I come home stressed out and tired from work and sometimes Marianne says something and it's just all I can do not to go off on her. That one time, I just lost it. I don't want to be like that anymore."

He got up from his chair and started for the door. Then he stopped and turned around.

"This is a pretty good job you got here, doc," he said, "sitting in this nice office talking to people all day. Must be the easiest thing in the world. Bet you never get stressed out, do you."

Anyone who thinks being a therapist isn't stressful just hasn't tried it. Despite Sonny's view that we have the least stressful job in the world, the evidence suggests that therapists are at risk for occupation-related difficulties given the ambiguous nature of our work, the possibility of vicarious trauma, and the vicissitudes of emotional labor (e.g., Radeke &

Mahoney, 2000; Rosenberg & Pace, 2006). How do therapists stay afloat emotionally amidst these stresses? More to the point, how do we flourish and provide the level of care for our clients that we believe they deserve? There is a growing body of research suggesting that mindfulness can be a critical resource in doing so.

Therapists' Stress

The sources of stress in therapists' lives are many and well-documented. We enter our profession with hopes of making important differences in the lives of the clients who seek our help (Rønnestad & Skovholt, 2003; Skovholt & Rønnestad, 2003). We quickly find that this achievement is not as straightforward as it seems. Clients come to therapy with a variety of motivations—often conflicting, and not all of them for healing. Those mixed motivations make the road to change rocky, twisting, and some-times even a dead end. And when clients do experience positive changes while in therapy, it is hard to know what part our efforts played. The clients themselves may not give us credit, not so much because they think we didn't help—although that can happen, too, of course—but usually because they don't realize we need their feedback to know that we made a difference.

When clients do confide in us honestly, we hear difficult stories. I still remember the first time a client told me about a murder he had commit-ted. I also recall sitting with another client as he struggled to reconcile the fact that his act of maiming a store clerk's face with a broken beer bottle had brought him help that made his life better. In both cases, and in so many more in my career, my job was to find a way to connect with the persons in front of me, to find their vulnerability, and what I could of their humanity, and resist the urge to distance myself from them when hearing the horrific events they had been part of. Over time, these experiences begin to eat away at our souls a bit. The technical terms are "vicarious traumatization" (McCann & Pearlman, 1990) or "compassion fatigue" (Figley, 2002) and they describe a situation where therapists and others who care for traumatized people begin to experience some of the same cognitive, physical, and emotional symptoms as their clients. We've all had that experience to some extent—the client you can't put out of your mind at the end of the day, another client's vivid description of abuse that keeps popping up in your thoughts. To do this work well, we have to connect with our clients; and to connect with our clients we have to be available to all of their experiences, not just the happy or easy ones. The more consistently we work with traumatized clients or hear traumatizing stories, the more vulnerable we become to compassion fatigue.

Despite the ambiguous nature of our work, and the level of difficult things we are witness to, on the surface, Sonny still seems to have a point.

Almost all of our work is simply having conversations with people. What can be so hard about that? Mann (2004) describes therapy as part of a larger category of occupations that involve "people work," where the main focus is interacting with other people. For therapists, interaction is almost our exclusive focus and we frequently interact with our clients at the deepest levels of emotionality. Ellen Baker (2003) writes, "Our work can be intensely demanding, frustrating at moments, and sometimes terrifying" (p. 3). In addition to the content of what we experience, being a psychotherapist also demands that we manage ourselves in line with the expectations of our profession. Among other things, this means that we must suppress the expression of some emotions while actively expressing others in the course of our interactions with clients. Failing in either direction can have significant implications for the well-being of our clients, and ourselves.

I recall meeting years ago with a couple—Allison and Doug—whose two young children had just been diagnosed with cystic fibrosis. The session was emotionally wrenching as these two people began to grapple with the fact that their children would face an ugly, progressive disease for the rest of their lives. I felt tears come to my eyes as I thought of their kids—whom I had also seen—and what the future held for them. But my tears had to be put away for the time being lest they divert me from being emotionally available to Doug and Allison or leave them thinking they had to moderate their own grief to somehow take care of me. We ended our session and I went on to my next client, Maria, who was raising her grandson, a boy nearly the same age as Allison and Doug's son. Maria was incensed that her grandson wasn't doing his homework the first time she reminded him to do it.

"I have to check on him all the time," she said. "I don't know what's wrong with him. I think he is just a bad boy."

Coming from the emotional intensity of Doug and Allison's pain, I found myself angry with Maria. How could she be so petty when the world could change her grandson's life in a flash? Why didn't she hug him for being the good boy he was 90% of the time? But, of course, I couldn't say it. To do so would have threatened the alliance I had with her and would have only driven her away from the help that might, over time, allow her to be more flexible and appreciative of her grandson. I swallowed hard and did my best to empathize with her. I had to suppress an emotion I was feeling at the time—anger—and do my best to find the roots of another emotion that I wasn't feeling—empathy. This careful management of our emotions is something that sociologists call "emotional labor" (Hochschild, 1983). In some jobs, workers do it because it is an expectation of the position—salespeople are often expected to treat us nicely regardless of what they feel or how we act in order to make the sale. In the helping professions, however, we engage in emotional labor because we believe it is in the best interests of our clients. It becomes a strong expectation we hold for ourselves. Doing so has positive outcomes for our clients; they need to hear the parts of us that value and care about them and not the parts that are sometimes bored or angry or distracted. Emotional labor also rewards us. When we successfully manage our emotions in a session, we have a feeling of mastery, of a job well done. When we don't, we have a sense of doing something wrong and not serving our clients effectively.

While emotional labor can be a satisfying part of our job when we perform effectively, it can also be a source of stress. We experience *emotional dissonance* when the emotional demands of an interaction don't match what we are truly feeling. This happens all the time for us in therapy. We regularly interact with clients who deserve our best empathy and concern, and yet we find we don't care for them much. We may be counting the minutes until the session is over while the client is telling us something quite important to her. On other occasions, we may find ourselves sexually attracted to clients who have been hurt and misused sexually in the past. It can feel almost as if we are victimizing the client again, even if our feelings are never directly communicated. And in general, we are expected to remain calm, provide leadership, and be rational in the midst of emotionally challenging and chaotic situations regardless of whether we are terrified, overwhelmed, or disgusted.

There are two ways that people deal with emotional dissonance in their work. One is to simply fake it. We act like we are feeling the appropriate feeling even if we are not. There is nothing wrong with faking it from time to time, especially if it is done in good faith on behalf of the client. For instance, we might act impartial as a client describes her plan to spend a weekend in a distant city with a man she has met over the Internet, even though inside we are screaming, "Don't do it!" Our impartiality helps the client more easily consider the pros and cons of her plan, instead of having to defend herself. With a boring client, we sit forward, nod more frequently, ask clarifying questions, all in an effort to communicate an interest the client dearly needs that we don't truly feel at the moment. Faking it can come from a deep concern about our clients. I'm sure all of us have faked it on occasion—at the end of a long day, or during the last session before vacation. However, a steady diet of faking it can lead to depression, cynicism, and alienation from our work (Ashforth & Humphrey, 1993) and is also associated with *depersonalization,* one of the three characteristics of burnout (Brotheridge & Grandey, 2002). Depersonalization occurs when we begin simply to go through the motions in an impersonal and largely unfeeling way. Therapy hours take on a lifeless and depleted character, becoming something to tolerate rather than something to invest energy in. I think there are times when faking it may be the best we can offer our clients, and is decidedly better than expressing the disinterest, anger, repulsion, or panic it is keeping at bay. Making a habit of faking it, however, can lead to burnout for us and lack of good care for our clients.

A second strategy for dealing with emotional dissonance is called *deep acting* (Hochschild, 1983). In deep acting, instead of faking it, we make an effort to actually have the feeling that is appropriate at the time. Instead of *acting like* we are interested in a boring session, we do our best *to be* interested. Hochschild suggests two approaches to deep acting—actively attempting to produce or suppress an emotion and the thoughtful use of imagination. Sometimes imagination can be useful. I went to my practicum supervisor when I was a student and said that a client was "11 on a scale of 10 of everything that rubs me the wrong way about people." I wanted the case transferred to someone else because I spent most of the session with this client being inwardly critical of him, even as he talked about his divorce ("No wonder she left him," I said to myself) and job loss ("I'll bet he drove his boss crazy").

"Try this," my supervisor said. "Next time you see him, imagine that he's just been diagnosed with a terminal illness. See if you can understand all of his difficult behavior as a reaction to this terrible news."

I was skeptical, but I agreed to try it because I was pretty sure my supervisor wouldn't transfer the case until I had. To my surprise, it helped. I was able to begin seeing my client as a scared, struggling man instead of as someone who came to therapy just to irritate me. While he wasn't truly dying, the insight still held true—he was scared and struggling. He didn't stop irritating me completely, but I was able to better connect with the more vulnerable part of him that the irritating behavior served to cover.

We don't use this kind of imagination much in therapy—at least, I don't. Instead, we have paid more attention to the other aspect of deep acting. Much of supervision is intended to help us understand the obstacles that get in the way of genuine and appropriate encounters with clients. We consult a peer or a supervisor if we begin to experience feelings for a client that could interfere with therapy. Instead of simply acting interested with a boring client, we try to figure out what about ourselves, or the client, keeps us from being interested. We try to understand our own emotional triggers, our family of origin patterns, or the stresses and struggles of our current lives, all in the service of removing obstacles to being truly present.

A significant body of research suggests that emotional labor is a source of stress across many professions that engage in people work. In fact, emotional labor can be as tiring as physical work (James, 1989). I believe this is certainly true of our work as therapists. We walk a fine emotional line hour by hour. We must become connected enough to our clients to truly understand their experiences, but we must not become so immersed in their emotional world that we lose our ability to see beyond the limits of what our clients experience so that we can help move them out of the difficult emotional situations they find themselves in. We must hold our clients close but not too close, necessitating a certain level of detachment. Maintaining that stance is hard work.

What Can Mindfulness Contribute?

What do we know about the usefulness of mindfulness for therapists? First of all, we know that it can be a good way to manage stress. Several studies show that mindfulness training results in a reduction in anxiety and depression, mood disturbance, and general stress for therapists and other caregivers (Beddoe & Murphy, 2004; Hassed, de Lisle, Sullivan, & Pier, 2009; Minor, Carlson, MacKenzie, Zernicke, & Jones, 2006; Rosenzweig, Reibel, Greeson, Brainard, & Hojat, 2003; Shapiro, Brown, & Biegel, 2007; Shapiro, Schwartz, & Bonner, 1998). Shapiro and her associates (Shapiro, Astin, Bishop, & Cordova, 2005) found that an 8-week mindfulness course reduced perceived stress, and increased self-compassion, for health care professionals. The increase in self-compassion is especially important since it seems to be a better predictor of emotional resilience than self-esteem (Neff, Kirkpatrick, & Rude, 2007).

In addition to helping with general stress, there is also evidence that mindfulness can combat the deeper stresses of compassion fatigue and burnout. Cohen-Katz et al. (2005) found that a mindfulness-based stress reduction intervention reduced nurses' scores on two of three subscales of a measure of burnout. Those nurses who took the mindfulness course reported decreasing their feelings of emotional exhaustion and depersonalization—both components of burnout. (While they also reported an increase in their sense of personal accomplishment in their work, this change did not reach statistical significance.) Harrison and Westwood (2009) interviewed six acknowledged "master therapists" who in the views of their peers excelled at working with traumatized clients. When these therapists were asked what allowed them to "sustain their personal and professional well-being, given the challenges of your work" (p. 203), one of the things they described was the importance of mindfulness, especially developing mindful self-awareness. How was it beneficial? The therapists that Harrison and Westwood interviewed suggested several ways that mindfulness helped them. They felt their mindfulness practices helped them by keeping them calmer and more grounded in the face of emotional intensity. These therapists, in other words, believed that their mindful awareness kept them more anchored and less reactive with their clients. Certainly, this on its own would be quite a benefit. But mindfulness also served as a support for some of the other strategies they used to maintain vitality in their work. It allowed them to have a much more finely tuned awareness of their own emotional boundaries and a stronger sense of when they were not maintaining enough emotional separation from their clients' experiences. Being present without becoming overwhelmed is one of the fundamental duties we have as therapists.

Mindfulness also helped these master therapists tolerate another common experience in therapy—ambiguity, when we lack control over the outcome and often can't tell for sure what real impact our efforts have. And moment-by-moment awareness contributed to their ability to be present for their clients and to engage in another of the factors that they felt shielded them from vicarious trauma—that is, *exquisite empathy*. Interestingly, in this group, empathy for their clients' experiences was not seen as a risk factor for vicarious trauma if it occurred in the context of clear boundaries that kept the therapists from fusing with, or becoming overwhelmed by, the stories they heard. When they were able to closely attune to their clients, they saw the benefits and this sustained them. Finally, mindfulness helped these clinicians remain hopeful even in the face of the suffering they witnessed—a key element in preventing burnout.

Although no one has studied it per se, we can hypothesize about some ways in which mindfulness can help with the stresses of emotional labor that therapists experience. I believe this happens primarily in Hochschild's realm of deep acting. Two factors seem to be at play. First, the work that my colleague Diane Gehart and I have done (McCollum & Gehart, 2010) suggests that mindfulness meditation helps therapists develop and maintain therapeutic presence with their clients. Geller and Greenburg (2002) describe therapeutic presence this way: "an availability and openness to all aspects of the client's experience, openness to one's own experience in being with the client, and the capacity to respond to the client from this experience" (p. 72). Being more present, and having a way to nurture and produce that level of presence, can reduce the need to fake it, with the attendant risks of depersonalization and burnout. In our study, our students, who served as research participants, noted that they often meditated before and after sessions as a way to increase their sense of presence.

A second aspect of mindfulness practice that can help with deep acting is by reducing reactivity. In *Buddha's Brain* (Hanson & Mendius, 2009), Rick Hanson uses our growing understanding of brain functioning to suggest a scientific basis for what meditators have experienced for centuries. What is clear is that mindfulness practice works to develop an area of the brain called the *prefrontal cortex*. This area inhibits emotional reactions that originate in the lower brain structures. It also helps us see the potential emotional rewards or costs of various courses of action and then make a choice about which to pursue. Strengthening the ability of the prefrontal cortex to observe and mediate emotional responses will support that aspect of emotional labor that requires us to *not express* certain things we feel and think while working with a client. If we are more aware of our emotional reactions and thereby able to decide which ones to express and which to withhold, we can act with more intention as therapists. Without this ability, we are much more likely to be simply at the mercy of our reactivity. The more energy required to manage our emotional reactions, the more depleted we can feel and the less likely we are to be present for our clients. Mindfulness practice appears to have some benefit for therapists, then, in dealing with the stresses that arise from emotional labor.

There is a final question to ask about mindfulness meditation for therapists. Does it result in better outcomes for our clients? We are only in the early stages of exploring this question. Escuriex and Labbé (2011) reviewed what research there is about the connection between therapists' mindfulness practice and client outcome and concluded that the jury is still out. Some studies find that mindfulness seems to increase therapist traits like empathy and therapeutic presence that are associated with good outcomes. Others do not. Some find a positive relationship between therapist mindfulness and others do not. There is one stronger study that does suggest that therapists who meditate have clients with better treatment outcomes. Grepmair and his colleagues (2007) examined the difference in clinical outcome between the clients of therapists who were practicing Zen meditation (closely related to the kind of mindfulness meditation we have been discussing here) and therapists who were not meditating. The therapists were randomly assigned to either a meditation condition or a control condition. One hundred twenty-four inpatients—divided between the meditating and nonmeditating therapists—were followed and assessed. The group treated by the meditating therapists reported a subjectively better outcome than did those treated by nonmeditating therapists. In addition, the patients of the meditating therapists showed greater symptom reduction on eight subscales of the Symptom Checklist (SCL-90-R) as well as on the Global Severity Index of that measure. Obviously, one study cannot completely answer the question of the link between therapist mindfulness and client outcome and we must await further, strongly designed studies to provide a more definitive answer. However, this evidence is encouraging and we might be able to assume that therapists who are less stressed, more present, and more vital in their work with clients will be able to help their clients have better outcomes.

5

CULTIVATING MINDFULNESS

Arthur fairly crackles with energy as he sits down on the edge of the chair in my office. His face is a little flushed and, I suspect, from the pattern of our previous six sessions, that he is primed to launch into another monologue.

"Doc," he says. "You won't believe it. You won't believe what Maureen did this time."

Today's story looks to be long and intricate, crowded with details, condemnations of Maureen (Arthur's ex-wife), and justifications for why he had no choice to act as he did, which, in this case, meant yelling at her in front of their kids when he came to drop them off after a weekend visit.

"I'm tired of being the good guy all the time," Arthur says.

Although it is hard for me to see how Arthur is being the good guy, I let him go a little longer because I have learned that he resists efforts to change the direction of our conversation until he has had some time to vent. As he talks, I find my mind wandering. I know it's the end of the month and time to do billing statements for all of my clients, but there's a show on TV I'd really rather watch instead tonight. But when will I get the billing done? Arthur continues, apparently unaware of my internal retreat. His flood of words leaves me feeling distant from him, uninvolved in his story, and frustrated that I haven't been able to help him turn the focus more on himself, more on something he has a chance to change.

As I notice my attention drift away from what's happening in the room in front of me, I take a moment and bring my focus to my breath. It is a familiar, centered place, one I go to often throughout the day as I find myself preoccupied or mentally absent. I breathe quietly for three or four breaths, feeling the gentle swell of my chest as I inhale and a bit of relaxation as my lungs empty.

"Be here," I say silently to myself. "Just be here."

I turn my attention back to Arthur just as he pauses for a second.

"You know," I say to him. "I think you must get really sad when you have to leave the kids with Maureen at the end of a visit. I think maybe you're a little scared, too, scared that you're losing them somehow when you don't see them every day."

Arthur stops. I can see the small glint of a tear in his eye.

"Maybe you got something there, Doc," he says. The briefest moment of silence. "But it would sure help if Maureen would quit filling their heads with lies about me . . ."

And the moment of connection is gone. But I've felt it and I know Arthur has too. We can come back here. I focus again on my breath.

"Be here patiently," I say to myself. "Patiently."

I credit my mindfulness practice with helping me walk the fine line between observing my inner world during sessions while still remaining present with my clients. I also believe it has helped me be more patient with the process of therapy; I'm less inclined to rush things when they shouldn't be rushed. I could have tried to push Arthur back to that moment of sadness, for instance, but I doubt that it would have worked. And it might have strengthened Arthur's defenses against letting anyone see his vulnerabilities. Better to be patient, knowing that we have made a connection and that the softer side of Arthur will emerge again. Like everywhere in life, it is tempting as a therapist to try to hang onto the moments that we value and push away the moments that we don't. I truly believe my mindfulness practice, and the experience of equanimity that has developed from it, help me in these potentially difficult therapeutic situations. Another way to think about equanimity is the ability to recognize when the doing mode of mind is not appropriate for the situation and then to be able to switch to the being mode.

But what do mindfulness practices look like? In this chapter, we will talk about how to cultivate mindfulness through breath meditation. Elsewhere, I'll also talk about other formal practices—walking meditation, for instance—as well as the importance of bringing mindful awareness to everyday activities. Before we begin, however, I want to talk about how to set the stage for practice, regardless of what form it takes.

Setting the Stage for Practice

Intention

It is important that we bring to our practice a vision of why we are practicing. Without some broad notion of the purpose behind our efforts, it is easy to lose motivation and wander away when the going gets tough. Jon Kabat-Zinn, a pioneer in bringing mindfulness practices to Western health and mental health care writes: "Your intentions set the stage for what is possible. They remind you from moment to moment of why you are practicing in the first place" (1990, p. 32). Think for a moment about why you are practicing mindfulness, or why you are considering doing so. Many of us begin with the wish for meditation to help with day-to-day issues—reducing blood pressure without medication, managing anxiety, improving our ability to stay present and focused in therapy sessions. These intentions are important and good places to start. Shapiro (1992) found that as time passed, however, these initial intentions broaden from wishing for a change in day-to-day life issues to wishing for greater self-understanding and eventually self-liberation. The important thing is not where we start. The important thing is that we remain cognizant of our intention for practice so that we don't lose our bearings when the practice is challenging.

Process Versus Outcome

One of the most confusing things I heard from my teachers as an early meditation student was the notion that mindfulness is not about trying to get somewhere. In other words, it isn't about an outcome. That seemed to conflict with the idea that we remain aware of our intention for our practice. I had a lot of outcomes I was hoping for—less anxiety, a calmer presence as a therapist, some more clarity about spiritual matters. As time went on, however, I came to understand that being tightly focused on the outcome of a particular meditation session or experience could begin to get in the way of pursuing my intentions. It's confusing, I know. After all, if we want something important, we usually pursue it with great effort and energy, redoubling that effort if we don't succeed at first. So I would begin a meditation experience with my focus on a desired outcome—keeping my breath in perfect focus, sitting stock still until the meditation bell rang at the end of the sit, and so on. Of course, I never reached any of those goals no matter how hard I tried. The more I "failed" the more effort I applied, and when that didn't help, the more discouraged I became. It wasn't because I was a bad meditator. It was because my focus on the outcome was getting in the way, making me worry about what I wasn't accomplishing rather than on what was present in each moment. So while we need to keep our intentions for our practice in mind, we also need to hold them lightly, without expecting that we will make incremental progress toward a goal every session or that meditation will always result in our feeling calm or relaxed or some other desired way. Here's where our training as therapists can help us. In therapy, we're used to separating content and outcome from process. Likewise in meditation. Instead of pushing ourselves toward a particular outcome, we can think about the process of our mindfulness practice. A process goal is something that we can always come back to regardless of the outcome. Being present with what I am experiencing is an example of a process goal. Noticing when my focus has left my breath and bringing it back is another. Treating myself with kindness during this meditation experience is also a process goal. These goals allow us to start over again and again, regardless of the outcome, and that is what much of meditation practice is about. They also help keep us from getting lost in comparing mind states ("I'm a failure as a meditator. Everyone else is surely doing this right") or dragged out of the present ("This whole session is going to be a waste if I can't keep my focus for even a minute"). For me, it was most helpful to take a simple, straightforward process goal into my early meditation sessions. For breath meditation, the goal can be, "Back to the breath." That is, each time you find your attention drawn away from the breath, release the distraction and come back. You will do this hundreds of thousands of times in your practice and it is easy to become discouraged because it doesn't seem like you are making any progress or getting "better" at being a meditator. But it is the *process* of coming back to the breath again and again that strengthens concentration and builds awareness of what is happening in our experience now in the present. As that concentration and awareness grow, they will allow us, when we are off the meditation cushion, to react to life in radically different, and more useful, ways.

Kindness. Mindfulness practice seems to work best when we approach it with an attitude of kindness for ourselves. We tend to hold ourselves to standards of perfection that, just as we discussed above in terms of outcomes, can make it hard to reap the benefits of mindfulness practice. Using a process orientation to our practice can help us develop that kindness. Each meditation experience gives us countless opportunities to realize our imperfections and return to the task at hand. Our attention wanders, and we bring it back. We itch when we wish we didn't. We have angry feelings toward people who don't deserve them. We pray for the bell to ring and end this practice that we entered into voluntarily with evidence it would be good for us. Without a measure of kindness, the practice can become onerous and discouraging. At its most basic level, I believe that mindfulness is first and foremost a practice of compassion and kindness. As one of my meditation teachers told us as we were preparing to leave a weeklong retreat and return to our daily lives, "You will need to forgive yourselves 10,000 times." It is some of the best teaching I have received. To find kindness in our practice, I think it can be helpful to adopt a phrase I have heard Jon Kabat-Zinn say over and over again as he leads meditations. The phrase is, "As best you can." We can only do the best we can at this moment under this set of circumstances. Expecting less of ourselves leads to a lackluster and empty practice, while expecting more leads to frustration and discouragement. Kindness comes when we find satisfaction in doing the best we can.

No "Correct" Outcome

As I teach mindfulness to my graduate students, I hear them saying over and over again early on, "I must not be doing this right." Most often, they're concerned that they aren't reaching a certain state during their practice sessions. We talked at the beginning of Chapter Two about the cultural ideas we have about what meditation practice entails and what it should produce in us. What are we to think when our meditation sessions aren't filled with resplendent light, or fulfilling peace, or amazing spiritual insights? What do we do when we find ourselves bored and restless during meditation? Or find our minds singing along to a popular song or worrying about making a grocery list when we should be focused on the breath? (I once made the mistake of listening to a CD of Willy Nelson's greatest hits on the way to a weeklong meditation retreat. I like Willy Nelson, but I thought my mind would never stop singing "Luckenbach, Texas" during the first couple of days of the retreat!) The easiest conclusion to draw is that we're not doing it right. If only we could do better, we wouldn't have these unwanted experiences. The problem *is* us, in a way, but not how we think it is. We aren't doing something wrong. Rather, we've become attached to a narrow set of outcomes and are dissatisfied when we don't reach them. This wish to achieve states we want and avoid states we don't is just part of human experience, of course, and we'll talk more about it later in the book. For now, let's just remember that in mindfulness practice, the goal is to be present with *whatever* is happening, whether or not it's a desirable state.

We could talk for hours about mindfulness and the components of this practice but, in the end, mindfulness is something to be experienced rather than learned about cognitively. So, let's begin with an experience of breath-centered meditation. I recommend that you use the associated soundtrack when learning breath meditation because there are a number of instructions that can help along the way and they will be hard to remember on your own. However, I am including a written version of the instructions here if you would prefer to read them and then try breath meditation on your own.

Breath Meditation

Preparation: In this exercise, we'll introduce the traditional breath meditation where the physical sensations of breathing are used as an anchor. Before beginning, it is useful to experiment with where to best pay attention to those sensations. There are three places where most people find it easiest to focus on the breath—in the belly, in the chest, and at the nostrils. We'll take a moment to try each.

The belly. Take a couple of deliberate breaths and notice the movement of the belly as you inhale and exhale. It can be helpful to gently place your hand on the belly as you do so. As you inhale, the belly expands, growing round and full. And then as you exhale, the belly contracts and sinks a bit as air is expelled from the lungs. Practice a few times to see if you can feel the physical sensations of that movement.

The chest. A second place where many people notice the sensations of breathing is in the chest. Bring your attention to the chest and take a couple of deliberate breaths. Notice how the chest expands and lifts a bit when you inhale and how it falls back when you exhale. You may even be able to feel this sensation in your back as the lungs expand against the back rib cage and the spine. Again, practice a few times to see if you can feel the physical sensations of breathing in the chest and upper body.

The nostrils. A third place that people use to focus on the breath is at the nostrils. This is a bit different than a focus on the belly or chest because there is less physical movement to focus on. Instead, the focus is on the movement of air in and out of the nostrils. You may feel the inhalation as a slight sensation of coolness as the air enters the warm body and then a gentle brush of air across the upper lip as you exhale. As you did before, take a few moments to try noticing the breath at the nostrils.

Regardless of where you are noticing the breath, do your best not to breathe on purpose. Instead, as best you can, let the breath happen naturally. This can be difficult at first, but noticing the breath is not a deep-breathing or relaxation exercise. In fact, the voluntary/involuntary nature of the breath provides a good laboratory to learn the concept of *allowing* without interfering. We can certainly make ourselves take a breath on purpose (the doing mode) or we can simply allow the breath to happen on its own (the being mode). Learning to focus on the breath without forcing it to be a certain way is a good introduction to accessing the being mode.

This practice takes a good deal of compassion. We easily get caught up in the notions of "doing it right" and usually assume that we are being successful only if we are able to maintain an unwavering focus on the breath. It really isn't possible. The mind is designed to be active, curious, and alert. While we can certainly gain a great deal from developing a stronger ability to focus, doing so takes practice. In fact, the "active ingredient" in meditation practice, so to speak, is not just the ability to focus. It is also the ability to notice when we have been distracted and then to bring our attention back to the anchor. Each time we notice our attention is elsewhere from the breath is a moment of awakening and each time we gently bring our focus back to the breath, we strengthen our concentration.

All right. Let's begin.

Begin by finding a comfortable posture. The important thing is that your back is straight but relaxed and that you are able to breathe freely and without obstruction.

We will begin by arriving in the present moment, purposefully taking a breath and bringing attention into the room with us. Noticing sounds. Noticing smells. Noticing the temperature of the air.

41

And then when you are ready, bringing your attention to your breath. Noticing the physical sensation of breathing wherever it is most vivid for you . . . at the nostrils, in the rise and fall of the chest, or in the movement of the belly. Taking a few moments in silence to simply experience the physical sensations of breathing.

As you notice the mind wandering from its focus on the breath, notice for a moment where it has gone . . . and then, with gentle kindness, bring it back to the breath. Know that the mind wandering is not a sign of failure or doing it wrong, but is simply part of what minds do naturally, what we want them to do so that they remain curious and active and engaged . . . And doing our best to bring compassion to this process.

And now sitting silently for a few more moments. . . . Noticing the cycle. . . . Focus . . . Distraction . . . Recognition. . . . Return . . . as it repeats over and over again . . . all of it held in a cradle of compassion.

*****

Take a moment after your breath meditation to reflect on what you experienced. Let yourself be open to whatever happened. You may have experienced a sense of peace and relaxation or you may have found the effort to focus on the breath frustrating. At times the breath becomes very subtle and doesn't provide a strong stimulus for focus. In these cases you will likely find your mind wandering off into past memories, thoughts about the future, or even things that seem nonsensical. On the second day of a weeklong retreat, I found myself becoming more settled and at peace in the mid-morning meditation. My breath was deep and regular. The back pain I usually struggle with for the first few days of a retreat had eased. I was sitting quietly, gently opening my awareness to whatever arose, when suddenly the thought popped into my mind, "I wonder if Betty Crocker was bisexual."

It took all my self-control not to burst out laughing and disturb the other retreat participants around me. As I calmed down, however, I was amazed at what my mind could create as a distraction when all I had asked it to do was to follow the breath and be open to whatever experiences it encountered.

The Next Step

Breath meditation is a version of concentration practice and one of its outcomes is to focus the mind and develop concentration. Each time we notice that the mind has wandered and we bring it back to the breath, we strengthen our concentration and focus. We also become a little better at observing our experience, a little better at noticing what's happening in our experiential world. Better concentration and a growing ability to observe what we experience represent the first steps in mindfulness practice and are ones that we can spend months and even years developing. While these practices can give rise to very pleasurable states of mind—calm, peaceful, expansive—they also serve as a foundation for the second component of mindfulness practice—*vipassana* or insight practice. Insight practice involves widening attention to observe whatever arises. However, without a sufficient foundation of concentration, the mind will be too distracted to be present.

Insight practice involves looking deeply into the nature of experience. Earlier I said that I found it useful to have a simple, process-oriented intention to give structure to formal mindfulness practice. As we begin to experiment with insight practice, I want to suggest such a structure for you to try that involves asking two questions:

What is happening in this moment?
Can I hold it with compassion?

These questions point to what are often called the two wings of mindfulness—wisdom or clear seeing, and compassion. How do we approach these questions in our own practice?

We can begin to approach the question of what's happening in the present moment by paying attention to three components of our experience—physical sensations, thoughts, and emotions. We might think of these as the basic building blocks of experience. We have already experimented with focusing on the physical sensations of breathing during breath meditation. We can expand the field a bit now to look at physical sensations in general. As we let our attention move through the body, we can focus on whatever physical sensations are present—tension, relaxation, pain, comfort or pleasure, warmth, coolness, whatever is present. While we may be able to discern a variety of sensations in various parts of the body, it is also a common experience to find areas of the body in which we are not able to feel much of anything. Not to worry. Without sustained practice in focusing on physical sensations, almost all of us have this experience. We just don't take the time to notice what is going on in our bodies. Sometimes, we even actively avoid it.

Paying attention to thoughts can be challenging. We live our lives so completely immersed in thinking that it is hard, at first, to find a vantage point from which to observe our thinking process. A good place to start is to simply notice the activity of the mind. Is the mind busy and full of thoughts? Calm and serene with thoughts coming at a regular pace? Or is the mind sluggish with thoughts mired in a bog of fatigue? Of course, these are only a few of the myriad possibilities. Practice will help develop the ability to step out of our immersion in the stream of thought in order to observe it.

We often think of emotions as intense experiences—rage, despair, ecstasy. Certainly these things are part of our experience, but much of our emotional life is more nuanced and subtle. One of my teachers—Tara Brach—talks about internal weather systems. I find it a useful metaphor for observing emotions and mood. Ask yourself how your emotional weather is right now. Is it an emotionally bright and sunny day, or dark and foreboding? Are you in the midst of an emotional storm or in the calm delight of a pleasant day? Or is your emotional weather simply overcast, neither sunny nor on the verge of a storm?

Finally, we can pay attention not only to the *content* of our experience (physical sensations, thoughts, and emotions) but also to its *process*. When we do so, we notice that experience is always changing and that our attention to parts of our experience is equally variable. Thoughts come and go, and we discover, as we hone our concentration and calm the mind, that they do so much on their own. While we can steer our thoughts in a certain direction ("I need to plan what to make for dinner"), when we don't give the mind direction, thoughts don't simply stop. Instead, the mind continues to generate them, sometimes seemingly at random. ("I wonder whatever happened to my first grade teacher, Mrs. Wilson? And that kid that sat next to me in her class . . . what was his name?"). A variety of judgments about our experience can also come into play ("Why in the world am I thinking about that? I need to be more productive with my time. I could have been a great writer if I'd spent less time daydreaming . . ."). And just as quickly, that thought is gone and another takes its place. ("What year did Lewis and Clark start their journey?") The same is true for physical sensations and emotional experience. A sharp pain captures our attention only to fade from awareness as we hear an unfamiliar sound and immediately begin to generate explanations for it. Experience and attention are continually in flux.

Let's try a brief exercise in getting in touch with these parts of our experience. Again, I suggest you use the associated soundtrack but I will provide a written script as well.

* * * * *

What Is Happening in This Moment?

Beginning by paying attention to your posture: sitting or lying down in such a way that the body is supported comfortably and the breath comes easily.

Now taking a few purposeful breaths . . . noticing the rise and fall of the chest or belly, or the movement of air at the nostrils.

And when you are ready, bringing attention to body sensations. Letting your attention flow through the body like a scanner, simply noticing what is there . . . without trying to change anything. Noticing areas of tension if they are present. Areas of relaxation. The pressure of the chair or cushion against the body. Noticing the feeling of your feet on the floor . . . your hands resting in your lap . . .

And when you are ready, bringing attention to thoughts . . . to the activity of the mind. Is the mind active and filled with thoughts . . . or calm and relatively absent of thoughts? Are thoughts crowding your consciousness or moving at a leisurely pace? Is the mind filled with energy . . . or tired and sluggish?

Knowing that the practice is to, as best you can, simply notice without trying to change anything.

And when you are ready, bringing attention to emotion and mood. Noticing the internal, emotional weather. Is your mood bright and sunny? Cloudy? Stormy? Overcast and dull? Full-force winds of ecstasy or an emotional hurricane?

Now letting your attention broaden to observe the play of attention and experience . . . noticing whatever is present . . . physical sensation, thought, emotion . . . how each arises, comes into the foreground of experience, builds in intensity and then begins to subside . . . sometimes the process taking a few seconds and other times the process taking minutes or even hours.

Now ending this experience with a return to a focus on the breath for a few moments.

* * * * *

Checking in regularly with these three components of experience can be a good way to strengthen our ability to know what is happening in this moment. But how do we hold what we find with compassion? For me, the primary component of compassion when it comes to our own experience is *acceptance*. And in my experience, there are two aspects of acceptance—one more receptive and one more active. The receptive aspect involves being open and present with whatever arises without trying to change it. There are generally two ways that our minds get involved in trying to change our experience: they either want to hang onto pleasant or desirable experiences, or push away unpleasant or undesirable experiences. This is such a fundamental part of how we operate that even saying it out loud sounds obvious. Of course we want more pleasure and less pain in our lives. Acceptance asks us to take a different stance. One of my friends a long time ago referred to this part of mindfulness practice as "watching the parade." Imagine that you are standing on the curb as a parade passes by. You don't have to do anything. The parade comes to you. If you grew up in a small town in Iowa as I did, the parade starts with the Boy Scouts' color guard, followed maybe by the mayor sitting in the back of a convertible, the city council riding on a hay wagon, next perhaps the high school homecoming queen on a float or the Chamber of Commerce president driving his restored Corvette, and then the high school band doing their best to stay in step, and so on. As bystanders, our only job is to experience what comes along the parade route. The parade moves at its own pace; we can't stop it or speed it up. We also take the good with the bad. Sometimes the band is a little off key, and if it stops in front of us to play a tune, we sit through it. And when the hardware store employees whiz by performing precision marching formations on riding lawnmowers (I'm not kidding about this), we wish they would stop right in front of us to put on their show. And that, of course, is the problem when we apply the parade metaphor to our own lives. We want to hurry through the unpleasant parts and hang onto what's pleasant. Acceptance helps us resist this urge as best we can, knowing that we will give in to the temptation again and again. In the process, however, we learn more and more about how the mind works.

In Western culture, acceptance can seem like resignation. The band is playing out of tune and it stops in front of us. There's nothing we can do about it except resign ourselves to our fate . . . "Stars and Stripes Forever" played a little bit off-key. How do we balance the idea of resignation? That's the second component of acceptance—bringing active engagement and curiosity to our experience. While the receptive aspect of acceptance helps us accurately perceive what's happening without interfering with it, the active aspect leads us to investigate our experience more intimately. Let's see how this might work.

Working with physical discomfort is a good way to practice bringing curiosity to our experience. Despite how comfortably we try to arrange things, formal sitting meditation is usually accompanied by some kind of physical strain. I tend to tense my back as I sit—one expression of striving to do it right, typically—and after a time this leads to muscle tension and some pain. The receptive aspect of acceptance leads me to do my best neither to resist the pain, nor to encourage it for that matter. As we let pain be, we can also begin to investigate it. With pain and other unpleasant experiences, the trick is to become curious about something we typically try to push away or get rid of. Can we move toward it? Can we bring focused attention and curiosity to the pain? Much of what we fear about pain exists on a conceptual level—that is, it exists in what we *think* or *anticipate* about pain, how long we fear it will last, what we think it will develop into. Investigation means setting those thoughts aside to become curious about the actual sensations that we label "pain." Where are those sensations specifically located? What space do they occupy in the body? What is their character—throbbing, aching, constant, variable, sharp, or dull? What thoughts and emotional reactions accompany them? Rather than simply resigning ourselves to painful sensations, can we look at them as important parts of our experience that can teach us more about how our minds work? If we can do this we notice a couple of things. First, we often notice that the sensations are quite variable and transient. Language—labeling a set of sensations "pain"—creates a kind of monolithic and unchanging vision; our pain will always be here in the same way. Investigation, however, reveals that most of the time physical sensations ebb and flow both of their own accord and in response to the kind of attention we give to them. The second thing to notice is that when a strong sensation—pleasant or unpleasant—appears in our experience, the mind often contracts around it. That is, when we feel pain, the mind devotes a lot of energy to dealing with it, usually by trying to fend it off. Pain becomes the focus of our experience. It's a hard concept to describe in words, but part of acceptance is to see if we can notice the rest of the space in our minds, the rest of the space in our experience, and enlarge the mind to contain an unpleasant experience without letting it dominate. Doing so can reduce the suffering associated with unpleasant experience. If we dissolve a teaspoon of salt in a glass of water (the contracted mind), the water tastes very salty. But if we dissolve the same teaspoon of salt in a gallon of water (the wide mind) the salt doesn't disappear, but the water tastes much less salty. In part, the extent to which unpleasant experiences trouble us has to do with the way we hold them.

While pain provides a good example of how to investigate our experience from a position of engagement and curiosity, investigation is also important when it comes to pleasant experiences, the ones we'd like to hold onto. It is equally instructive to see where we experience pleasure in our bodies, what thoughts and emotions are part of that experience, and how our minds also contract around what's pleasurable. Once we have a hint that something is pleasurable, we begin to want more of it, to want it longer, and we begin to anticipate its end, which leads to its own kind of suffering. I once left the Barre Center for Buddhist Studies in Massachusetts after an intensive study course that had significant periods of meditation. As I drove along the wooded roads leaving the center, I tuned the radio to a classical station and found that it was playing one of my favorite pieces of music. It was nothing short of a magical experience. The drive was beautiful, the music matched the experience perfectly, my body felt whole and filled with peace. When I stopped at a roadside store to get gas and something to drink, I had a lovely interchange with the woman behind the counter—an interchange filled with ease and humor. It wasn't long, however, before I began to wonder, "How can I make this last? Maybe this is the way life will be from now on. . . . But what if it isn't?" Soon I had lost the magic of the moment—a moment that became magical simply by my being fully present—and I was deep in a tunnel of worries about what would come next. Pleasurable experiences provide us a different challenge because we don't want to dilute them in the larger mind, we don't want to see their variable nature, their ebb and flow. Yet, seeing that even pleasures come and go gives us a measure of equanimity.

Pleasures come and go and we do our best if we enjoy them fully while not clutching them too tightly.

The receptive and active aspects of acceptance work hand in hand to create a richness of experience that neither one could create on its own. Long before I had much experience with mindfulness, I remember going to a party and noticing a woman sitting quietly in a chair against the wall. She had a kind of blank look on her face, her eyes were a bit unfocused and downcast, and she sat without talking to anyone around her or moving much. All this while music played, people were talking and laughing, and the party swirled around her.

"What's with her?" I asked someone.

"She's into mindfulness," was the reply.

"My god, who'd want to end up like that?" I thought to myself.

Of course, I don't really know what was going on for the woman at the party, but I imagine she had adopted the receptive aspect of acceptance as something of a creed and was missing the active engagement part. In my view, mindfulness shouldn't leave us on the sidelines. Maybe if we were committed to life in a monastery with the cultivation of meditative insight as our primary goal, such a stance would make sense. But for those of us who live in the nonmonastic world, mindfulness—the active, and accepting engagement with our experience—should take us into the heart of life while helping us maintain a foundation of equanimity. We certainly can watch the parade when we need to, but we also need to step into the street and be part of that parade. The mindfulness parade includes the whole breadth of human experience—love, misery, anger, sorrow, sex, ecstasy, satisfaction, ennui. Grab your trombone or xylophone and march along.

A final word about acceptance. Accepting our current experience and engaging it with curiosity can be a true path toward more freedom and equanimity. However, it does not mean that we put ourselves in danger or tolerate external situations that are harmful. It doesn't mean that problems such as abusive relationships, being bullied, or severe medical problems for which there is treatment, are to be tolerated. I like to tell my students that Buddhists run out of burning buildings like everyone else and then try to put the fire out. They don't sit in meditation posture trying to experience burning. However, when it's your mind that is on fire, there's no place to run, and then the skills of acceptance, curiosity, and the wide mind can bring some measure of peace.

6

THE COMPLEXITIES OF COMPASSION

"What I regret most in my life are *failures of kindness*. Those moments when another human being was there, in front of me, suffering, and I responded . . . sensibly. Reservedly. Mildly."
(George Saunders, quoted in Lovell, 2013)

There seems little doubt that compassion is fundamental to the enterprise of therapy (Gilbert, 2010). It's hard to imagine a psychotherapy that would ignore compassion—that sense of concern and kindliness we expect from those to whom we turn for help. We might even think of compassion as one of the core elements of therapy going back to Rogers' (1957) definition of the necessary and sufficient conditions for change: positive regard, genuineness, and empathy. That certainly sounds like compassion. Without these conditions, therapy is at best superficial and, at worst, harmful.

Some years ago, I was in therapy for a time with a therapist who, I ultimately decided, just didn't like me. Our hours together weren't awful—there were moments of intensity—but the overall experience was, at best, lackluster. Despite a good enough start, a subtly critical tone crept into my therapist's work with me over time. I came to therapy in the midst of a personal crisis that had caused me to lose my emotional bearings and left me more vulnerable than I'd felt in years. The confidence I had had was gone and I was mistrustful of my instincts in most situations. As I tried to put my suffering into words, I began to experience my therapist as bored, or irritated, or simply struggling to stay present as I talked. When I raised issues of concern, she didn't seem to get what I needed from her and I often left feeling diminished instead of heartened. Her responses left me wondering what it was I was doing wrong, and what about me kept her from being on my side, why she quietly edged away from my suffering.

I've been a therapist for nearly 40 years now and I'm a pretty savvy consumer of health care services. If I get to a doctor I don't like, I go somewhere else without wasting much time thinking about it. I try to keep myself informed about what's new and current in health issues that affect me. In my own therapy, however, it was very difficult for me to really understand what was going on. The experience was subtle, and it hit me where I felt weakest, in my own faltering sense of who I was. In this atmosphere, when my therapist intimated that I was too emotionally closed down—which was likely true given my circumstances—therapy became not a search for liberation on my terms but a performance in which I tried hard to be who *she* thought I should be—more emotional, more dramatic, even more entertaining. When nothing seemed to work, I terminated, I think to both our relief.

I actually did get some help from that therapist. But when I began therapy a year or so later with a therapist whose warmth and liking were palpable, only then did I realize what had been missing in my previous therapy, and how much more I might have profited had it not been for what I can only describe as a failure of kindness. But there are often not remedies at the time because it is such a difficult thing to grasp. As a friend and colleague said as we were discussing this issue, "A failure of kindness can be so quiet and so subtle, and perhaps then so easy to excuse."

What's So Hard About Compassion?

I think we have erred in our discussion of compassion, both as a profession and as a society. We speak of it offhandedly, as a given, as if it is a state that should arise naturally, without complication. In my experience, it isn't so. And our failure to acknowledge the complexities of compassion complicates things more, making it harder to talk about those subtle failures of kindness that undermine our efforts to help the clients who come to us. What makes compassion so complex? First, we need to understand what it is. Many things masquerade as compassion. And then we need to find the courage to face where true compassion takes us. Those can be scary places indeed.

What do we mean by compassion? In Buddhist psychology, compassion has a very clear meaning. Compassion is the ability to feel the suffering of another being along with the wish to lessen or eliminate that suffering. That seems straightforward enough. When we see a hurt child crying, we're moved to pick her up and comfort her. When I realize I've forgotten to feed the dog and she is hungry, I give her food. And I'm convinced that one of the most difficult things in life is when we see the suffering of a loved one—a sick child, an aging parent—and cannot ease it. When we can't ease another's suffering, it troubles us. But let's dig a little deeper. On what basis do we perceive the suffering of others? One way we might experience compassion is through sympathy, that is, imagining ourselves in another's shoes. This is not an insignificant act. We must first pay attention to those around us, perceive their suffering, identify with it, and wish to help it end. I think this is often what we mean when we discuss compassion as a general term. But it leaves out a core aspect of compassion from the Buddhist perspective, namely our shared humanity as the basis for compassion. Sympathy suggests the ability to empathize with a *separate* other. Compassion occurs when we see deeply enough into the world to recognize that we are all fundamentally connected and that my friend's suffering isn't just his state of being that I can relate to; it is my suffering, too. Paul Gilbert is a psychologist who has put compassion squarely in the center of his approach to therapy. He says of compassion that "its essence is a basic kindness, with deep awareness of the suffering of oneself and of other living things, coupled with the wish and effort to relieve it" (Gilbert, 2009, p. xiii). Compassion means we need to know our own suffering if we are to feel compassion in a way that connects us to others rather than resting in a sense of separation.

It is a daunting task we take on as therapists, to know our own suffering along with that of our clients. The obstacles to knowing our own suffering are myriad. The wish to avoid pain is so basic that it seems inconceivable to even question it, despite the fact that avoidance often leads to more trouble. We also have cultural views that suffering is shameful, occurs because we are imperfect or have failed in some way, or that if therapists have problems they should only be problems that are neatly tucked away in the past, already solved. Touching our own suffering does not come easily.

This Buddhist definition of compassion challenges us in another way. It challenges us to see the *connection* with our clients who are suffering, to see our shared humanity. In some way it is only by chance that they wear the label of client and we of therapist. They, like we, are doing the best they can in this moment to be happy.

For some clients, feeling our shared humanity isn't much of a stretch. We meet clients who are much like us; clients who we would likely have as friends had we not met them professionally first. For other clients, it is not so easy. We're eager to see the differences between us, eager to stay separate and distant. Sometimes it's because those clients reflect back to us parts of ourselves we don't like—the lonely child we once were, the cheating spouse who reminds us of the part of ourselves that dreams of running away to a different life. Sometimes we struggle because our clients frustrate us or are simply not very pleasant people, at least on the surface. And sometimes our clients scare us. When I worked with adolescent boys in the hospital, assaults on the unit were not unheard of and I helped wrestle more than one kid into restraints. Most often, though, it isn't physical danger we fear, it is the emotional places our clients need us to visit with them. I've worked with a variety of people over my career whose common humanity felt deeply buried—murderers, psychotic patients, those with drug addiction or histories of prostitution who did unimaginable things out of desperation. I must admit that feeling our common humanity was scary with many of them because it made me wonder what I might be capable of, and what I might do, if faced with the same situation. Sometimes I pulled back, much as I tried not to. I hid behind the distance that professional roles and credentials create for us. But when I managed to stay present, I think the rewards were great.

I was taught the healing power of shared humanity a long time ago by a patient called Artie. Artie was schizophrenic and hospitalized on the inpatient unit where I worked at the time. At times chastened and subdued by his auditory hallucinations, Artie could also be exuberant and full of energy, seeming to say whatever thought came to his mind. He was in therapy with a staff psychologist who shared a waiting room with the therapist I was seeing at the time. As I wrote earlier, it was not uncommon for those of us on the staff to run into clients in various waiting rooms as we both awaited our own therapy appointments. Usually when we met patients under those circumstances we would politely acknowledge one another or do our best to be unobtrusive. Not so with Artie. The first day he saw me waiting for my therapy session he came right over and sat down across from me.

"What are you doing here, Dr. McCollum?" he asked me.

Taken aback a bit by his question, I said the only thing that occurred to me: the truth.

"I'm waiting to see my therapist," I told him.

A quick wrinkle of confusion spread across his forehead.

"Your therapist?" he said. And then a broad smile as he looked at me in a different light.

"Hey, Dr. McCollum, does that mean you're screwed up, too?"

It became something of a touchstone for us. Artie would see me from time to time in the halls and ask, "You still screwed up, Dr. McCollum?"

"I'm working on it," I'd tell him.

"Me, too," he'd say. "Me, too."

The day Artie was discharged he called me from the unit phone as he was on his way out.

"I'm getting out," he said.

I told him that I knew he was being discharged and wished him good luck.

"You know," he said, "it was great to know that staff had problems, too. I didn't feel so weird." He paused for a moment. "I hope you get better soon."

Although it sounds funny, it was, in fact, a touching moment. Despite all that might be used to set us apart, Artie and I were simply two human beings, each trying to solve our problems. Our problems were certainly different in character, but the process was the same; we were both engaged in the human struggle for happiness, and it helped to connect us.

It sounds so simple—but human connections can be fragile. What keeps us from making connection? In Buddhist psychology, there is the concept of far enemies and near enemies. A far enemy is the opposite of the emotional state we seek, and is usually readily identifiable as not the desired state. For instance, the far enemy of compassion is hatred or cruelty. Few of us would delude ourselves into thinking that we are feeling compassion when we are filled with hate for the other person. The distinction is clear. Near enemies are harder to identify. The near enemy of compassion, for instance, is pity. Pity feels like compassion because we see the suffering of another and wish it would stop. However, pity differs from compassion in a fundamental way. Pity sets us apart from those around us, and usually sets us above them. We feel their suffering based on the premise that we have something that they do not. We have peace of mind while they lack it. We are healthy and they are sick. They are dying and we are not. Of course, if we look more deeply, we see that that premise is a false one since our peace of mind can evaporate in an instant, our health can decline, and we are, in fact, closer to death every moment we are alive. It's also hard to be the object of pity. There is something demeaning about being helped by someone who sees himself as superior to us even when the help we receive may be sorely needed, and much appreciated. True compassion in therapy allows the client to receive the help she needs without having to surrender her dignity or humanity in order to do so.

Fears of Compassion

It would seem, from all the good that comes from a compassionate stance in relationships, that compassion would flow freely in our lives. But we know that isn't true. We all experience anger, frustration, separation from others, and a host of other emotions that keep us from feeling compassionate. I've already described some of the struggles we have with compassion—confusing it with sympathy or pity and the way in which it brings us face-to-face with our own suffering. In addition to that, however, many of us have fears associated with compassion. Gilbert, McEwan, Matos, and Rivis (2011) describe three sources of fear about compassion—fear of feeling and expressing compassion for others, fear of receiving compassion from others, and fear of having compassion for ourselves. Some of our fears about compassion come from societal beliefs and attitudes about compassion and what a sense of community entails. Other fears may be more personal, based on our personal experiences in relationships, perhaps the result of the failures of kindness George Saunders wrote about.

I believe that most of our fears about compassion play on an under-lying feeling of vulnerability. When we think about fears of feeling compassion for others, we worry that feeling compassion will make us vulnerable in ways that will lead others to take advantage of us. It's not an unreasonable concern. We've all had experiences wherein our efforts to be kind to a friend or family member, or maybe even a psychotherapy client, lead to more and more demands until we have to end or severely limit the relationship and weather the accompanying anger and disap-pointment. Alternatively, we may fear that if we are seen as compas-sionate, we'll also be seen as a "soft touch," someone who is easily manipulated. In part, this fear comes from another misunderstanding about what compassion is. Compassion is not without boundaries and our compassion for others has to be balanced with care for ourselves. Having boundaries and paying attention to one's own needs can be seen as antithetical to compassion, but it isn't so. Part of being compas-sionate is knowing what is good for us as well as what is good for those around us. Compassion isn't about always being soft and yielding; it also demands strength and force at times. Preserving our own integrity allows us to continue to be compassionate without having to retreat and regroup if we become depleted, thereby abandoning the person who is the object of our compassion.

Another aspect of the fear of feeling compassion is that doing so may seem to violate our Western ideals of autonomy and independence. We hold strong cultural beliefs that people should make it on their own, without undue help from others. Compassion leads us to want to ease the suffering of others, but our culture says they're responsible for solving their own problems. Healthy compassion depends upon accurate discern-ment. We need to be able to see when helping directly to relieve suffering is the best course of action or when encouraging the autonomy of the other is best.

We had a client being seen in our campus clinic who had come for a number of months. She was habitually late for sessions, often canceled at the last minute, complained about the amount of money we were charg-ing her, criticized the therapists who worked with her for their efforts to help, and spent many of her sessions lying on the love seat in the therapy room with her eyes closed, answering most questions in monosyllables. She really was in desperate straits with no job, a husband whom she basi-cally supported, and a history of very difficult experiences. Her therapists had tried a permissive and seemingly supportive stance with her, allowing her to lie on the couch, miss payments on her bill, and come late or not at all as was her wish. As time went on, however, it became clear that this stance wasn't helping. She remained stuck.

When I started supervising the case and a new therapist began working with her as the semester schedule changed, we decided a new direction was needed. Her new therapist began to ask the client what she wanted to get from coming to therapy.

"That's a stupid question," she said. "If I knew that, I wouldn't be here, now would I?"

The client called me after that session to complain that her therapist was too young to really help her and that asking her about goals for treatment wasn't useful.

"I've been a therapist for more than 30 years," I told her, "and I always ask my clients about their goals." She hung up. But she continued to come to sessions.

The therapist told her that she needed to come regularly, and on time, if therapy was going to help and that if she missed more sessions we would have to think about giving her time to someone on the waiting list.

"It's the bus schedule," she said. "The damned buses don't run on time."

"Maybe you need to take an earlier bus," the therapist said.

The client made a face but the next session she was only 5 minutes late, not her customary 20.

Next the therapist set some limits about the fee. "You need to pay us something every time you come and some of it needs to go toward the balance you owe us."

The next session the client arrived on time and the change in her appearance was remarkable. Where before she had been generally unkempt, she now wore a clean, pressed blouse. She had combed her hair and used a little make-up.

The therapist acknowledged the change and asked what was different.

"I found a better bus," she said, explaining how she had arrived on time. There was a pause. "You know, I need some better buses in my life."

There are times when making allowance for clients makes sense. Someone deeply grieving may need flexibility in our expectations, for instance. But in this client's case, we weren't expecting enough from her. When we began to expect more, she began to make changes in her life. The trick is not to let ourselves become so angry that we respond punitively. It takes a clear mind to discern what we can do that will be the most helpful in any given situation.

Finally, we can fear that being compassionate toward others serves to let them off the hook for bad behavior. How can we feel compassion for someone who has wronged us, or wronged others, without somehow excusing their behavior? Shouldn't people suffer for their misdeeds? It is a complicated issue. At our training clinic we use one-way mirrors to observe our students as they work with clients. We also have intercom phones to call in to the session and speak to the student, suggesting a specific intervention or a different direction to take the session. I recall watching a student once as a relatively self-centered client began to see the impact her behavior had had on those close to her. She was talking about how she had stolen money from a family member.

"You know," she said, "that was a really bad thing to do."

The student quickly replied, "Oh, I don't know that it was that bad."

There are a variety of critiques we might have of the student's response but the one that struck me most was how he dismissed an important insight that the client had, one that could lead her to a different way of being with the people in her life. We had a long talk about it after the session. He believed that being a compassionate therapist meant stepping in to reassure people whenever they talked about difficult issues or suffering. But in this case, doing so left little room for the client to explore a newfound insight. Sometimes compassion means accompanying the clients as they experience the difficult things they need to experience, rather than trying to short-circuit the process. Coming in contact with our suffering in the short term may set the stage for relieving much more suffering in the long term. I don't think this is letting them off the hook, although it is different than punishment, which entails trying to increase the other's suffering. Sometimes compassion calls for us to simply be with what is and recognize that we, too, have hurt other people, behaved badly, and have things in life that we regret, maybe serious things. We come to our clients from our shared humanity.

While feeling compassionate toward others can arouse fears, so can having others express compassion for us. We need to understand these fears both for our own sake and to better understand some of the difficulties our clients face and the ways they insulate themselves from the very compassion they so desire.

For some people, recognizing the compassion others feel for them can lead to feelings of increased vulnerability, or even shame. Since pity is often mistaken for compassion, it is easy to feel that those who hold us with compassion see us as diminished in some way, and that wanting others to be kind to us is a sign of weakness. Others are reluctant to be seen with compassion because they don't trust it. I don't know how many clients over the course of my career have told me stories of needing to feel the kindness of those close to them, only to be disappointed. Sometimes there was frank aggression, but more often there was a bland response, a deflection, a dismissal. I recall one client telling me how he had, as a young adult, gone to his parents to explain that his youthful—and very troubled—marriage was coming apart and that he was thinking seriously of divorce.

"Well, I don't know what you want me to say," his mother said, missing the efforts he had made to make it work and the anguish in his voice. "Don't you want to save your marriage?"

"All I wanted," the client said with tears in his eyes, "was for her to say she was sorry that I was hurting so much, that she knew it must be hard. But she couldn't."

He was quiet for a long time as he relived the scene in his mind and I could see the waves of hurt cross his face. Failures of kindness leave a mark. How do we trust expressions of compassion in the present when they were so disappointing in the past?

Another fear associated with feeling that others see us with compassion is the fear that we don't deserve it. It becomes difficult to reconcile how others see us in a positive and forgiving light when we aren't able to do so ourselves. Under extreme circumstances, compassion can even become painful. I once worked with a man, Evan, who came to treatment after he participated in a crime that left another man crippled. By being in treatment, he was able to avoid a jail sentence. Early on, Evan was angry and resentful of our efforts to help him. He challenged the rules, sat silently in group, and was generally contemptuous of our efforts to help him. Gradually, however, we began to recognize his suffering beneath the façade of anger and, as time went on, we were able to touch it. Having someone be kind to him was a new experience for Evan. And it was not always an easy one. I vividly recall a group session where he said, "I'm here because I crippled someone and being here is the best thing that has ever happened to me. But how do I deserve getting something this good after doing something so bad?"

How do we deal with the fears of compassion? One antidote is self-compassion. According to Germer (2009), self-compassion is the ability to "bear witness to our own pain and respond with kindness and understanding" (p. 1). Self-compassion rests on a foundation of mindfulness: the ability to accurately perceive our internal states and to be with them without judgment. Self-compassion is an antidote to the harsh, critical inner voices that many of us struggle with—voices that express beliefs about us so extreme that we would never express, nor likely even hold them, about a friend. Self-compassion is also an alternative to self-esteem. Self-esteem is based on self-evaluation, the value we place in ourselves. Self-esteem can be fragile since any indication that we are not valuable has to either be resisted or must erode our sense of self-esteem. Kristin Neff (2009)—one of the primary scholars of self-compassion—notes that in Western culture we often base our self-esteem on how different we are from others and typically on the degree to which we are superior to them. Like the children of Garrison Keillor's Lake Wobegon, we must all be above average, and any threat to our standing—a failure, something we just aren't good at, someone's criticism of us—must be either challenged or denied. The continuing need to prove our worth may also lead us to distort our perception of ourselves to keep any hint of imperfection at bay.

Self-compassion, on the other hand, isn't based on having a particular set of attributes (beauty, wealth, power, fame), nor is it based on being better than others. Indeed, like compassion for others, compassion for ourselves is based on the recognition of our fundamental humanity and that we deserve compassion for that fact alone. We aren't better than others but are connected to them, connected to the basic human struggle for peace and happiness. Self-compassion allows for compassionate recognition of failings or "deficits." Indeed, deficits recede in importance when we no longer need to compare ourselves to others. We can rest in a sense of acceptance, able to forgive ourselves when we stumble, and not needing to continually strive to be other than who we are.

There is a growing body of research literature that points to a number of positive outcomes associated with self-compassion. MacBeth and Gumley (2012) conducted a meta-analysis—combining the results of 14 studies and 20 separate samples—to examine the relationship between self-compassion and what the authors labeled "psychopathology," primarily depression, anxiety, and stress. Higher levels of self-compassion were associated with fewer psychological symptoms. Further, this was a strong relationship, leading the authors to conclude that "compassion is an important explanatory variable in understanding mental health and resilience" (p. 545).

Despite the evidence that feeling compassion for ourselves is useful and restorative, reluctance to feel it remains. It seems especially hard for therapists, whose orientation is primarily taking care of others. I don't know how many times in leading compassion meditations (I'll describe and give direction for this later), therapists and therapy students want to skip the part about offering compassion to themselves and move on to offering compassion to others. But if we aren't truly compassionate for ourselves, how can we be compassionate to others? If we haven't experienced the fears and struggles that stand in the way of being compassionate, how can we help others work with them? What keeps us from seeing ourselves compassionately?

One fear about self-compassion is that it will make us soft, as if our standards for ourselves will fall and we will accept failings that we shouldn't. In this debate, the counterpoint to the voice of self-compassion is our inner critic. One of the first things that most of my students discover as they begin to practice mindfulness meditation is the nearly constant running critical internal commentary. Some of the criticism is leveled at others, but most of us find that most of the time we turn it on ourselves.

"That was a stupid thing to say. What will she think of you now?"

"You're no good at anything. Anyone could figure out how to change the ink in the printer."

"God, I look horrible. Who would want someone with his gut hanging out like this?"

Perhaps you can see the inner critic's connection to self-esteem. It tries its best to help us live up to the dictates of self-esteem by putting us on a track of constant improvement and the attempt to meet goals that are usually vague and therefore never met. The inner critic is also convinced that without its efforts, we will fail miserably, and it presents us with a variety of catastrophic scenarios about what will happen if we ease up on ourselves. My inner critic lives in constant fear, for instance, that without its vigilance I will somehow sink into abject poverty and find myself living on the streets of Washington, DC, at the mercy of the wily street people who will take every advantage they can. To combat this fear, my critic chides me when I don't work hard enough, with "hard enough" never being clearly articulated. It criticizes me when I spend money on things it thinks are frivolous, that is, things that bring me pleasure and are likely to distract me from "hard work." Finally, my critic absolutely throws a fit if I feel tired, or sick, or bored, and consider just taking some time to care for myself—a nap, a sick day, a walk outside on a beautiful day. Not working hard is courting disaster.

Mindfulness practice is a wonderful laboratory in which to examine the inner critic, its relationship to the ever-illusive self-esteem, and to develop more compassion for ourselves. What appears to be a ridiculously simple practice of paying attention to the physical sensations of breathing is actually amazingly challenging and gives us any number of ways to experience "failure." We find that we can't keep our focus on the breath for more than a millisecond. Our minds wander off into the strangest places. We itch. We adjust our posture one way and then another, never satisfied. We give up and abandon the session after 5 minutes. We forget to meditate, or we're too busy, or too stressed, or too distracted to do it. (One of my friends puts "meditate" on her daily to-do list to remind her to practice.) Each of these experiences is an opportunity to bring compassion to ourselves rather than bear the attack of the inner critic. Compassion is not about ignoring or failing to see ways in which we could do better. Rather, it is about accepting that, as human beings, we will always encounter things that don't go as we wish they might, act in ways that we wish we hadn't, don't accomplish our to-do list every day. We find that we have lost focus on the breath and can treat this either as an example of failure or we can bring compassion to it—recognizing that we are indeed upset by what has happened, that it is part of being human, and that we deserve to be treated with kindness in its wake. While losing focus on the breath may not be a source of intense suffering (although it can be), it does give us a way to practice this process and most especially to treat ourselves with kindness as we do. It can help us break out of a habit of mind that is deeply embedded in our culture. Kristin Neff told the *New York Times* (quoted in Parker-Pope, 2011): "I found in my research that the biggest reason people aren't more self-compassionate is that they are afraid they'll become self-indulgent. They believe self-criticism is what keeps them in line.

Most people have gotten it wrong because our culture says being hard on yourself is the way to be."

Another belief that interferes with self-compassion is the belief that others need compassion more than we do. This one seems particularly common among therapists. We tend to put others' needs—emotional and otherwise—ahead of our own, believing that it is selfish or mean-spirited to take time to care for ourselves.

A number of years ago I did a videotaped interview with a family that was designed to illustrate the issues facing families with chronically ill children. The tape was to be used for training students and practicing professionals and, after the work with the family was over, the producer interviewed me about what I had done. She noted that I paid attention to strengths in my talk with the family and that I tried to help them build on their existing strengths instead of looking only at deficits. When she asked me why I took this stance, I recall telling her two things. First, and most important, I do it because it is true. It is too tempting to see struggling families as only having problems and not having strengths as well. Failure to acknowledge those strengths does a disservice to families by not recognizing their resilience, as strained as it might be by circumstances. Then I added that I also did it because it makes my job easier, that using the strengths that clients bring means I don't have to work as hard and that I can preserve my own energy and investment in what can be very difficult work. The project had an advisory board comprised of family therapy educators who reviewed all the material before it was distributed. They asked the producer to take out my statement that focusing on strengths made our work easier. The implication seemed to be that it was illegitimate to do something because it benefited us in some way, even when the clients' needs were being met and being met well. We need to pay careful attention to this notion of self-sacrifice in our profession and counter it with compassion and care for ourselves. As therapists, we are the primary tool we use to help our clients. If we don't take care of that tool, it will fail and we either will become ineffective, or actually harmful.

Finally, there is another fear that can be associated with self-compassion. By being kind to ourselves, we fear we will unleash a torrent of strong and difficult emotions that have been kept at bay by a stoic and unemotional stance. Many of us invest a significant amount of emotional energy in avoiding certain aspects of our emotional experience. We actively try not to think about certain things. We may engage in driven activities like shopping, eating, sex, or drinking to distract us from unwanted thoughts or feelings. We avoid activities or people that challenge our emotional suppression. It can finally come to the point where even allowing a kindly feeling toward ourselves threatens the numbness that seems like the only refuge from what we believe we must put aside emotionally in order to survive.

A Catholic nun came to see me early in my career. She sat nearly mute in my office for several minutes as she struggled to begin to tell her story. After I asked a few gentle questions, she began to talk. She had had a love affair with a priest, a man with whom she worked every day. Although they both knew the affair violated their vows, and although they were both deeply religious, the depth of feeling between them was compelling. They talked about renouncing their vows and marrying. My client began to imagine what life would be like as a married laywoman. And then one day the priest came to her and said he had had a complete change of heart and that he was breaking off their relationship. His words were curt and cold. He said they were both sinners and seemed to blame my client for what had happened. But they continued to work together in the same office and saw each other every day. He refused to speak to her if he could avoid it in any way. He made sure to only be in her presence when others were around. He did his best to not even make eye contact with her. She had endured this for more than three months by the time I saw her.

She could hardly look at me as she talked and when she finished her story, she met my gaze with what seemed to be the expectation of condemnation.

"My goodness," I said to her, "how unbelievably terrible this must have been for you. How have you stood it?"

For a moment, she looked confused that I wasn't scolding her, and then she dissolved into the deepest sobs I have ever heard. Sadness, despair, shame; everything she had been trying so hard to keep at bay came pouring out. Just one small moment of compassion opened the floodgates, and began the healing.

It is hard to imagine psychotherapy without compassion, but I hope by now you also see that compassion is not uncomplicated. Holding others with compassion, or finding them acting toward us with compassion, can evoke a variety of feelings, from the secure and lovely sense of resting in the exquisite kindness human beings are capable of to taking us to some of our deepest sorrows. What does this mean? It means that we must consciously cultivate compassion, that it doesn't necessarily flow unimpeded. The next section describes a Buddhist approach to cultivating compassion.

Lovingkindness Meditation

Lovingkindness or *metta* meditation is a way to build compassion. The Buddha introduced *metta* meditation after sending his followers out into the woods to meditate. They returned saying that they were fearful of the tree spirits that haunted the woods. The Buddha taught the monks *metta* practice and sent them back into the woods. As the monks cultivated greater and greater levels of *metta,* the tree spirits were calmed by it and befriended the monks. I believe *metta* meditation, then, both helps us cultivate compassion and assuage the fears that might accompany our efforts to live compassionately.

The practice of *metta* meditation entails silently repeating a series of phrases that serve to offer lovingkindness to oneself and others, culminating with the offering of *metta* to all beings. In the traditional literature, there are four wishes one makes: to be happy, to be safe, to be healthy, and to be at ease. Being at ease connotes a state of equanimity where one accepts whatever comes one's way. Lovingkindness is usually offered in ever-widening circles of inclusion, beginning with oneself, then a benefactor (someone who has cared for you or helped you in some way), good friends, loved ones, then difficult people for whom offering *metta* is a challenge, and finally to all beings. I can't stress enough how important I believe it is for therapists not to shortchange time spent offering ourselves lovingkindness. Since we spend so much of our time caring for others, our first inclination is often to rush through caring for ourselves and move on to others. But as I noted above, time spent caring for ourselves is a necessary part of maintaining our ability to care for others.

* * * * *

Practicing Lovingkindness Meditation

Following is a guide to the practice of lovingkindness meditation. As with the other meditation practices, I encourage you to use the accompanying soundtrack to really guide you in this practice.

To begin, then, settle into a comfortable posture and calm the mind. Then begin repeating the following phrases:

> May I be safe
> May I be free from suffering
> May I be healthy
> May I be at ease

As you repeat the phrases you can picture yourself as you are now, as you were when you were a child, or even as you were at a time in your life during which you were most in need of lovingkindness. You can also visualize your heart as the seat of lovingkindness. Regardless of what you visualize, or whether you visualize at all, simply do your best to let yourself receive the wishes for safety, happiness, health, and ease that you are offering to yourself. *Metta* meditation is initially a concentration practice and you will find the same phenomenon happening that you find when you focus on the breath. The mind will wander. Just as you did during breath meditation, when you notice that the mind has wandered away from the phrases, release whatever thoughts or story you have been distracted by and bring the mind back to the phrases, starting over again with "May I be safe" if you can't recall where you left off. It is not uncommon for the phrases to seem rote and formulaic for periods of time just as the breath can seem dull and uninteresting. Continue to repeat the phrases nonetheless, doing your best to sense lovingkindness spreading throughout your body and gladdening your mind. You might begin with 15 or 20 minutes devoted to *metta* practice or you might begin and end a period of breath meditation with *metta*. For therapists in particular, it is important to spend several weeks offering lovingkindness to yourself until the feeling of kindness for yourself gains strength. The temptation will be to jump to "those who need it more than I do." Resist that temptation.

The next person to whom *metta* is offered is usually a benefactor. This is a lovely practice where you have the chance to symbolically repay someone who has helped you in life by offering them lovingkindness. Since mentor and benefactor relationships can be complex at times, choose a benefactor that you can wholeheartedly appreciate. There will be time later to work on offering *metta* to those for whom you have more difficult or conflicted feelings. As you find your heart opening to your benefactor, begin to expand the scope of your wish for well-being to friends, family, and other beloved people in your life. Finally, when you feel strong in your practice of lovingkindness, you might try offering kindness to difficult people in your life and even to your enemies if you have them, wishing that they might be filled with ease and well-being.

While *metta* practice is an important part of Buddhist meditation practice in general, I believe that it is of particular importance for therapists. We deal daily in the realm of hurt, suffering, and the need for compassion, and we face the fears and struggles of striving to bring compassion to our practice. We need ways to keep our hearts open and water the roots of compassion in our lives.

7

THINGS GET IN THE WAY
Obstacles to Being Present

I find myself dreading the hours I spend with Hector, a client I've seen four or five times. He hasn't been in therapy before and he struggles to put his inner life into words. When he does manage to communicate what he's feeling, it is a grim picture. He's at least moderately depressed, stalled in his professional life, angrily distant from his partner Manuel. I feel myself stiffening a little when Hector sits down. He usually sighs deeply and then looks at me with a sort of discouraged grimace on his face.

"What should we focus on today?" I ask him.

He shrugs his shoulders.

"Nothing's different," he says. Then silence.

I can feel a demand in the silence. Do something. Fix me. But Hector can't seem to tell me enough about his situation for me to really know what to do.

Hector provokes a variety of feelings in me. I find myself struggling to stay present with him, wishing I was seeing another client, subtly angry at him for making me feel so incompetent, sleepy, and bored sometimes when he does finally say a little about what is going on for him. And occasionally, his slow speech and long pauses make me want to jump up and run around my office screaming. At any of these points, judgment sets in. I begin to wonder what kind of therapist I am if I am feeling so distant and critical about a client. What kind of meditator am I if I can't seem to stay present for a simple conversation? The judgments make me even more uncomfortable and make it even more difficult to stay present with Hector, feeding the cycle even more.

Whether it is in meditation practice or in our therapy hours, we all encounter mind states that are difficult to accept and deal with and that serve as obstacles to being present. In Buddhist psychology, these are known as hindrances and the Buddha described five of them. Some of the classical names seem a bit archaic—ill-will, sloth and torpor, sensual desire—but the experiences are common. We find ourselves desperately not wanting what we have, desperately wanting what we don't have, bored and sleepy, restless, and plagued with doubt. While mild versions of these states may not be that troublesome, there are two ways that these states trap us. First, they can take us over, convincing us that they are what they say we are—enduring states of mind that we must take any action, no matter how unskillful, to avoid. When this happens, they become hard to see. They seem like they are just the way things are. Alternatively, we may recognize that we are caught in a difficult state of mind but then begin to battle it, trying to control, suppress, or avoid it in some way. In either instance, they stand between us and being present. The key to release from a hindrance is to do our best to look clearly at it, see the conditions under which it has arisen, and also recognize that it is a temporary state, arising and moving on like all other states of mind. We do this best in the context of compassion for ourselves, not blaming ourselves for what's happening but doing our best to accept it with curiosity and kindness. If we can resist the invitation to either fuse with them or battle them, they offer us avenues to deepen both our practice and our work with our clients. As we become more familiar with the hindrances, as we investigate them more deeply, we have the possibility of not having them visit as often, and of knowing better how to be with them when they do.

Desire

Grasping, clinging, and attachment can be troublesome experiences, but they don't necessarily have to be so. It is nearly impossible for most of us to go through life without preferences for how we would like things to be. In fact, our preferences serve us well if held lightly. They direct us toward the things in life that are important to us: working with skill and mastery, spending time in nature, loving our children and partners. When desire becomes obsessive, however, it begins to stand between us and being present. There are two ways that the hindrance of desire manifests. First, it can drive us into an overpowering focus on what we *don't* have. The more our minds suggest to us all the things we lack, the less able we are to see what is right in front of us, the things we *have*, the possibilities of the present moment, in other words. Desire in this form can leave us feeling bereft, wanting, full of longing, and absorbed in wanting to be anywhere but the present. I don't know how many hours I've spent during meditation retreats, for instance, wishing I was anywhere but on my cushion in a large quiet room with a lot of fellow meditators. But the more I wish that, the more I miss out on the rare gift that is a meditation retreat. We are so lucky to be able to use the support of our families, our workplace, our friends, and of the retreat leaders and staff to take an entire week to try to become more familiar with our own mind and the habitual ways in which it operates so that we may learn to be more present, more whole human beings. Wishing we were really at Best Buy picking out a new big screen TV takes us far away from the moment-to-moment arising and passing away of experience (although it is a little more complicated than that, since watching how easily we slip out of the present is incredibly instructive).

As therapists, we all encounter times when the client who is sitting in the office with us isn't the client that we wish was there. Hector, who I described at the beginning of the chapter, was that kind of client for me. As I struggled to be with him, a part of me wished desperately for a different client, one who was more verbal, forthcoming, more psychologically minded, and introspective. If Hector would only be that client, I told myself, then I could really do some good work. However, all the time I spent wishing Hector was different than he is was time I wasn't actually present in the room with him and that made it hard to truly make a difference as his therapist.

The other way that desire can manifest is in an attempt to hang onto something that is destined to go away despite out best efforts to keep it. And sadly enough, everything goes away. Just last night I was sitting and found myself struggling a bit. I was working to get back into regular practice after some weeks of not sitting regularly. My breath was tight and uneven, my mind bland and small. I did my best to bring compassion to these experiences and see if I could look more deeply into them. What I discovered was that I was trying to put myself back into the state of deeper concentration that arises more easily when I practice regularly. I found myself longing for the simplicity of the breath, the moment of deep peace after an exhalation and before the next breath arises, the sense of being settled in the body. But the more I grasped for this state, and the more I looked for little pieces of it that I clung to desperately, the more I struggled. When we try to hang onto desirable states, or to actively create them, we discover their independence. They come and go based on the conditions that give rise to them and our best bet is to get better at cultivating those conditions. The only real path to that kind of peace is to be with whatever is happening in the moment, desirable, not desirable, or simply neutral. Failing that, we are left frustrated, feeling out of control, and even plagued with self-blame. What did I do that made such good things go away? Clinging is, after all, an effort to be in control. And when our efforts fail, one handy surmise is that something is wrong with us.

In therapy, I often get caught in this trap after a particularly good session, especially with a client with whom I have struggled. When the client arrives for the next session, I'm usually hoping we can take up where we left off. It happened not long ago with Hector. For whatever reason, he came to a session more open, more talkative, more willing to share some of his vulnerabilities.

"This was a good session, doc," he told me as he left that day. I thought so too.

The next week, however, saw him back in his usual form, shrugging helplessly when I asked him where we should start the session and what seemed most important for us to talk about. Sitting silently as long as I did. Speaking only in short phrases as he tried hard to express himself. Knowing what he was capable of from the previous meeting, I redoubled my efforts. I asked more questions. I phrased them in different ways. I could sense my breath getting constricted and higher in my chest. I thought that there must be a way to help Hector get back to where we'd been last week.

Finally, he looked at me with exasperation.

"I just don't know," he said. "I don't know."

My intensifying efforts to help Hector return to a place that I wanted him to be, that we had both found helpful, actually served to push him away. I certainly wasn't present with him in our session. I was trying desperately to be present to the version of Hector that had been there last week. And I probably left him feeling deficient in some way as he sensed my struggle and knew he wasn't fulfilling my wish. Wes Knisker—a meditation teacher and author—said in a talk at a retreat I attended that we can spend so much time hoping to recreate the lovely states we experienced the last time we went on retreat that we miss what the current retreat is all about. The same can be true in therapy.

Momentary experiences of clinging and desire are inevitable and not terrifically harmful. And having preferences in life is not a bad thing, either. Not only is it unavoidable, but our preferences guide us and orient us toward what is important. When desire becomes paramount, however, or we find that we are holding so tightly onto things that are destined to come and go despite us that we are adding significantly to our suffering, then we may need to take a different stance.

How do we know that desire has overcome us? The metaphor of the South Indian coconut monkey trap is instructive. You construct the monkey trap this way. You cut a hole in a coconut that is just big enough for a monkey to slip its hand into but too small for him to withdraw a clenched fist. You put a rope around the coconut and stake it to the ground. Then you put some rice in the coconut and leave it out for the monkey to find. The monkey smells the rice, reaches into the coconut to grab a handful, and then can't withdraw his clenched fist. Because of the way monkeys are wired, they don't release the rice even in the face of the danger of being caught. The way to freedom is to simply let go of the rice. So we know that desire has overcome us when we cling to what we want to such an extent that it intensifies suffering and limits the life we are able to lead.

How do we deal with our hand caught in the desire trap? The first step, of course, is to recognize what's happening. It is so easy to be

67

seduced by the notion that if we only had the right object, the right state of mind, the right client, the right office furniture, the right *something,* life would be perfect. Or at least better. So we begin by recognizing that we're caught in a state of desire and we do our best to accept it. There is a strong temptation to fight it, to order it away, to judge ourselves for feeling something that is only human. Instead, we see whether we can hold that feeling with kindness for ourselves and look more deeply into it. The trick is to turn our attention from what we desire to investigate the *process of desiring.* During formal practice, we can investigate what desiring feels like in the body. What emotion or mood is nearby when we are caught in desire? Is desire a reaction to boredom? Does it arise in those moments when life feels empty or devoid of the meaning that enlivens us? Or does it arise when feelings of sadness begin to color our mood? In therapy, we can notice how desire takes us away from the present moment with the client, how it leaves us dissatisfied with what we have in front of us in the room and longing to be elsewhere either physically or emotionally, and how, as we move into the world of internal longing, we lose the ability to be with our clients in ways that promote change. We can also work with antidotes to desires, ways to develop our ability to counter unhelpful desire. One such antidote is generosity. Since desire encourages us to cling, to hold, to hoard both things and experiences, we can practice giving them away. In therapy, I think this means generosity of the spirit, rather than becoming so protective of what we want, to open more fully to the moment and try to be as present as we can with whatever arises. Sometimes that means sitting with boredom as a grieving client tells her story again. Sometimes it means playing a game of cards with a boy who can't yet tolerate talking when all we long to do is hear the story that will begin to help him heal. As therapists, simple presence is the best expression of generosity—simple presence and the compassion that comes with it.

Aversion

You know the signs. As a dreaded client's appointment time nears, you begin to look for the message waiting light to blink on the phone, hoping she'll cancel. You wonder if you'd be justified canceling yourself since seeing the client means missing the first 12 minutes of your daughter's soccer game. Or maybe the tickle in your throat is the beginning of a case of strep. Self-care is an ethical mandate, isn't it? And it is better to go home than infect your client.

"Don't you ever have a client you don't like?" one of my students asked me in class just last week. We'd been talking about being present and what we owe our clients—that is, our best effort to be with them. I realized maybe I'd been painting too rosy a picture. I've gone through

OBSTACLES TO BEING PRESENT

the little scenario above probably hundreds of times in my career. We all encounter clients that are hard to be with or who bring with them emotional states that we'd rather push away. One of my friends told me recently, after a long day of counseling difficult couples, "I don't know how much more acrimony I can witness."

Aversion arises when we find the world as we'd prefer it *not* to be and we want to push those unwanted experiences away. We strike out against what's present in this moment, declare it untrue, do our best to separate ourselves from it if it's our own state of being. This morning it was raining when I needed to walk the dog. She didn't want to wear her coat but I didn't want to smell wet dog all day. A part of me was irritated at the dog because she needed walking, as though the rain were her fault somehow. And I've long believed that she thinks the rain is my fault and that I could turn it off if I wanted. Instead of heading out open to the experience of a rainy morning, we both trudged with our noses out of joint through what would normally be an enjoyable walk. Aversion is the hindrance that challenges me the most. With some effort, I can at least temper my desires, generally energize myself, calm my restlessness, and continue to have faith in the practices of both psychotherapy and meditation. But turning toward the things I so desperately want to avoid just seems wrong. Like desire, aversion is an effort to control the unfolding of events and it feeds the illusion that if we push back hard enough, fight intensely enough, or run far enough, then whatever has arisen that we don't like somehow will not have arisen.

My experience with Hector is one example of how aversion shows up in therapy. At other times, we find ourselves averse not so much to the client but to the emotional states or experiences they bring with them. Grieving clients can be challenging in this way. They return week after week with the same difficult experience, with the need to tell their story over and over, and they wish us to bear witness to their suffering. It is important and necessary work but it can arouse a variety of feelings in us that we would prefer to avoid. Avoidance takes a number of forms. It takes my students a while to understand that reassuring clients often isn't helpful. With a grieving client, it is tempting to tell them that things will get better, that they will survive their loss and their lives will go on. Usually this is just our way of pushing away the depth of their grief. We may also encourage them to act, to do something, which can be important at times but we need to make sure we aren't simply trying to make the grief go away because we don't want to feel it. Researchers who study grief report that the bereaved consistently report certain responses from others that are not helpful to them. Advice-giving is one such response (Toller, 2011; Vachon & Stylianos, 1988). Also consistently reported are responses that appear to minimize the loss, or to urge the bereaved person to "hurry up and get over it" (Dyregrov, 2003; Ingram, Betz, & Mindes,

2001; Vachon & Stylianos, 1988). Our well-meaning efforts to make the grief better can actually leave bereaved people feeling misunderstood and more emotionally isolated.

Like all the hindrances, bringing mindful attention to the process can be extremely helpful. When we investigate aversion, what do we find? One thing to notice is how aversion orients us toward the doing state of mind when being may be a more functional approach. Our efforts to keep unwanted experience at bay often comes with a price. In meditation practice, we can become involved in an endless series of maneuvers to ease an achy knee (sit straighter, slump a little, move one knee, other knee now starts to hurt because of change in posture . . . and on and on) that takes us away from the simple experience of the ache and being with what is present in the moment. You also miss the chance to see that much of the suffering associated with pain comes from the mind and from the real physical sensations of pain. Here, we're like the child who begins to cry when the mere mention of a vaccination comes up and when there isn't a needle in sight. (Disclaimer here—I'm talking about working with simple and mild aches and pains. Mindfulness practice is not a form of masochism. Attend carefully to significant pain and don't ignore it. You don't gain anything by hurting yourself.)

A little deeper look at aversion illuminates our failing efforts to control things that aren't ultimately controllable. The weather is a perfect example. Despite my irritation with the rain and the dog this morning, all I could do was adapt. We both grudgingly put on our coats and I grabbed an umbrella and off we went. The inner experiential weather can be the same way. While we have the illusion that we can manipulate our moods and thoughts, they happen largely outside of our control. A bad night's sleep can leave us feeling foggy and unsure. A colleague's perceived snub can provoke a funk. Some random thought can flit through our minds and all of a sudden we are struggling not to laugh out loud in an important meeting. What's the experience of not being able to control the uncontrollable? We usually find fear. Are we simply at the mercy of whatever happens next? To some degree, yes. We can influence some of the conditions that give rise to events but we can't fully control them. Shy and awkward for much of my younger life, I've been trying lately not to retreat into my smartphone or iPad when I'm in a public place like a coffee shop. I try to make eye contact with the people around me and smile if it seems appropriate. In this way, I am making an effort to create conditions that cultivate connection. I get a lot of nice responses to my efforts but it doesn't work all the time and occasionally someone seems put off. I can cultivate the conditions for connection but I can't control the outcome. That can be a bitter pill the more precarious our emotional or physical safety feels. One outcome of this experience is that we blame ourselves. Surely if we were only smarter, better meditators, more accomplished therapists, taller, thinner, or something, we would be more successful at controlling what's around us. We come to feel like failures, like bad people, and that we have much to be ashamed of. Accompanying fear is anger, the energy of fear turned outward. According to Sharon Salzberg (in a wonderful series of four videotaped talks on the hindrances; Tricycle, 2011), in Tibetan practice, anger is understood as what we pick up when we feel weak because we believe it will make us strong. When we come face to face with our inability to control all of what happens to us, we become angry and that gives us a momentary feeling of strength. It takes a variety of forms—self-righteousness, blame, ill-will. What we find, however, is that the feeling of strength is illusory and the underlying fear comes back to haunt us.

As we discussed in the previous chapter on compassion, lovingkindness is an antidote to fear and thereby can be a way to deal with aversion. Instead of entering into the cycle of fear and anger, we can stop and offer lovingkindness both to ourselves and to the object of our aversion. Since aversion tends to separate us from things, we can try to recognize our connection even to the things that we dislike.

I think of desire and aversion as related hindrances in a way. Both are based on an effort to control our experience and reflect an underlying sense of vulnerability and fear that haunts us because we know, at some level, that life just isn't amenable to our control.

Hector is a hard client for me because he reminds me of myself, at other times in my life, when I felt lost, unable to ask effectively for help, and bewildered in the face of life challenges. His underlying sense of hopelessness scares me a little, too, because I have also been there. I'd like to avoid all of this but when I am in my best mind, I am able to offer lovingkindness both to Hector and to that younger self I see reflected in him. I try to remind myself that we are both human, both doing our best to live a life that can be confusing, daunting, even brutal. If I can hold onto that, I can also remember that this life provides us moments of exquisite beauty as well and hold for Hector the promise that he can find some of that beauty, too.

Sluggishness and Restlessness

Sluggishness and restlessness seem to share a focus on the energy of the mind and body and the relationship between the complementary forces of energy and tranquility. Sluggishness includes a physical sense of sleepiness, tiredness, even exhaustion, as well as a lack of mental energy and focus. Restlessness, on the other hand, includes physical agitation as well as anxiety and worry. While I am separating out the components of these states as physical or mental for the sake of description, it's important to keep in mind that the body and mind are intimately connected, and when closely observed the distinction between those two concepts begins to fall away.

We can cultivate presence with the right balance of energy and tranquility. Sluggishness and sleepiness are perhaps more difficult to deal with because they can masquerade as tranquility, although they lack the clarity of mind that is part of tranquility. In addition, they require a certain amount of discernment because there are different reasons we get sleepy and different approaches to them. According to the U.S. Centers for Disease Control, between 30% and 40% of U.S. adults report getting less than the recommended 7–9 hours of sleep (Centers for Disease Control, 2013). In addition, the pace of life and the level of stimulation in our culture add to a feeling of tiredness and depletion. Sleepiness may occur simply because we're tired and it emerges more strongly when we find a quiet moment. I often find myself rushing through the day feeling like I have plenty of interest and energy, and then fighting to stay awake when I sit down in the afternoon to read something, even when it's something I'm interested in. If sleepiness is truly the result of insufficient rest, it may make best sense to take a nap in lieu of meditating. On retreats, I often find that, on the first couple of days at least, a nap during the after lunch or mid-afternoon sitting practice session refreshes me enough to come back to the remainder of the day's practice with energy and focus. At other times, it makes sense to investigate sleepiness, especially when we are tempted to fight against it or when judgment is involved. Like each of the hindrances, we can do our best to bring curiosity and kindness to our experience, accepting it for what it is and seeing if we can become more familiar with it, not as a failure of some sort but as a way to learn more about the habits of the mind. On one retreat, I was struggling a great deal with sleepiness despite my strategy of napping in the afternoon. I found myself impatient, wishing that I could somehow overpower the feelings of fatigue and depletion I was feeling so that I could get to the "real" work of meditation. With coaching from my teacher, I tried my best to investigate what was going on. I certainly saw the influence of desire and aversion in my efforts to control the uncontrollable. But I also found that, when I approached sleepiness with some curiosity, I could see a fascinating interplay of sleep and consciousness and I could follow consciousness right to the edge of sleep, where I found I could make an actual decision about whether or not to go to sleep. In daily life, we don't usually have time to investigate phenomena in this depth, so our experience is that sleep simply overtakes us. When the hindrances become the object of attention, they can help us further our understanding in powerful ways. It is also possible to bring energy to our practice in other ways when sleepiness if a factor. It may help to meditate with eyes open, or to do walking meditation, or to simply meditate while standing.

Sleepiness can have a number of other functions when tiredness is not primary. It can create a sort of cozy state in which we can metaphorically curl up and let the world and our experience of it go past without truly encountering it. I think of it like the feeling of being inside on a rainy day where we may be warm and dry but we aren't really experiencing the weather. While this is pleasant, it subtly suggests that there are parts of the world that we should avoid. Sleepiness or apathy may also appear when we don't have a clear focus for our practice, as when we drift away from a focus on each unique breath to a more diffuse or random anchor. Apathy may also be an expression of boredom, and boredom is usually an indication that we aren't truly present, that our attention isn't truly focused.

Sleepiness and apathy can also be a way of avoiding what we find difficult. In Buddhist psychology, sleepiness is sometimes seen as a lack of the courage needed to be in the present moment. When we meditate, we may become sleepy in the face of a difficult emotional experience or even in the face of some of the initially unsettling realizations that arise as we look deeply into our experience. On a number of occasions on retreat, I've suddenly found myself face-to-face with the vast emptiness of life. As the retreat structure takes away the many strategies we use to avoid this realization—we don't talk, interact with others, read, listen to music, and so forth—being present with that emptiness feels like stepping off the edge of a cliff into the unknown. On more than one occasion, I've edged up to that cliff's edge and been suddenly overcome with tiredness and the need for a nap. Trusting completely that we will have what we need in the present moment is ultimately liberating, but taking the first step in that direction is truly an act of courage.

I think apathy or even outright sleepiness in therapy can serve the same function. Just as Hector reminds me of difficult aspects of my life I would rather forget, clients arouse a variety of states in us that are difficult. Numbing ourselves, letting the mind grow dull so that we don't have to bear the full impact of what we are experiencing, or longing for that cozy spot beside the fire instead of being present to the rainy day of emotion in the room are all ways to protect ourselves. The alternative is to trust that we have the skills and strength to be present. Being present is a challenge when it seems that the suffering before us will endure forever and we forget that even suffering comes and goes. However, there is inordinate power in being in the moment if we can find the courage to trust it.

Finally, we need to be sure that fatigue, apathy, and numbness aren't the result of poor self-care. Sometimes we need the equivalent of a nap as therapists. At times a quick "nap" is all we need—a walk outside to feel the fresh air and see the sky, a chat with a colleague or friend in the middle of the day. Other times we need a broader solution—time off from work, exercise on a regular basis, activities that challenge us in good ways apart from the emotional challenges of therapy, and, of course, regular mindfulness practice!

While sleepiness is a common experience during meditation, and apathy is its corollary in therapy, we can also experience the other end of the continuum when we find ourselves restless and having too much energy. Obviously, both physical and mental energy are useful while meditating and in therapy to keep the mind clear and engaged. However, when energy is not balanced by tranquility, it can transport us out of the present. Sometimes restlessness shows up as a primarily physical experience. In its milder forms, it can simply be a bit of a distraction. I sit in a wooden rocking chair when I work with clients and sometimes I find myself rocking away at quite a clip if I'm feeling restless. Sadly, my rocking chair tends to "wander" as I rock, and more than once it has come close enough to my bookshelf that it hits the stack of waiting-to-be read journals that seems perpetually there and triggers a mini-avalanche. More troubling is the feeling of inner agitation that makes us want to jump out of our skins. Restlessness also manifests itself psychologically, in what we might call the ruminating mind. Rumination leads us back over the same territory again and again without helping us find a way forward. I like to think of it as sort of mental quicksand, since the more we struggle with it, the more it seems to consume us. And we struggle with it because we are desperately wanting to grasp something to hang onto that will settle the thoughts and bring us a little peace. Toward the end of a retreat, I suddenly found myself ruminating about an issue that had come up at work in which I feared I had made a mistake that could hurt a co-worker. I thought again and again about the steps I had taken, unsure whether or not an e-mail had been sent just to one person or to several. Had it gone to several, my co-worker would likely have been quite hurt. There was no way to check what I had done while at the retreat and it took all of my dedication not to pack my bags and leave early to rush home to control the damage I was convinced I had caused. I sat the rest of the retreat flooded with fantasized catastrophes, recriminations, guilt, anxiety, and an endless round of replaying all my actions to see if I could convince myself that it would all be okay. When I did arrive home, I was quickly able to verify that I had not done anything wrong and the worries and ruminations all faded away like morning mist.

The ruminating mind can also take over our therapist selves. Sometimes this happens in the session, but I often find it extending beyond the boundaries of work, keeping me immersed in what I did or should have done, or in what I fear might happen in the future.

"Did I ask that client carefully enough about suicide?"

"Did I put him off when I tried to make that silly joke? Did he think I was laughing at him?"

"How will I deal with it if she comes back angry about our last session?"

"What would I do if he really tried to kill himself?"

As with all of the hindrances, restlessness takes us out of the present moment and away to the remembered past or the anticipated future. My worries at the retreat meant I had left the gathering psychologically long before my body drove home in the car. My worries about clients keep me at arm's length from my nontherapist life that can so nurture and refresh me and return me to my work with renewed interest and energy.

The first step to dealing with restlessness is to clearly recognize it and then to hold it, as best we can, with compassion. Ruminative thoughts tell us that they are true with great conviction and it takes effort and clarity of mind to step back and realize they are only thoughts, thoughts that may, *or may not,* be true. Can we bring curiosity to restlessness and discern its qualities? Once we separate a bit from the experience, we can bring two qualities to it. First, we can ground ourselves in the present moment. The body is a great door to the present so we can bring attention to physical sensations—the feeling of our feet on the floor, the cool air in the room against our skin. If restlessness is intense, walking meditation can be a skillful way to be with it. Walking meditation lets the energy move but also contains it in the structure of meditation. We can work to calm the body, consciously trying to soften the tension and agitation that are hallmarks of restlessness.

The second quality to bring to restlessness is spaciousness. Restlessness invites us to contract emotionally and to clamp down physically as if to contain the energy lest it escape our control and run amok. Attempts to shut down, however, have the paradoxical effect of increasing the tension. Now there is the force of restless energy against the force of our efforts to contain it. If we can hold restlessness in an expanded rather than contracted mind, we give it more room while not releasing it willy-nilly. In meditation practice, this may take the form of simply opening the eyes as a reminder of the big space of the world that surrounds our body that seems about to burst. Walking meditation can also calm the mind just as it calms the body, and sometimes simply going outside to feel the spaciousness of the outdoors in enough. Opening one's focus to the sounds in the environment also helps to create spaciousness. I've sat several retreats at a wonderful retreat center in the Virginia countryside that has a large, round meditation hall with screen windows on all sides. Listening to the calls of the birds around the hall has been a wonderful meditation on spaciousness as the calls—both lovely and harsh—erupt and then fade in the broad, open sky. While birdsongs in the country are certainly bucolic, I've also had the same sense of spaciousness listening to the electronic chime of the elevator down the hall from my office when

I've meditated at work. Sound is a pathway that reminds us of the spaciousness of the world, and of the mind. Thus we can both ground and expand in the face of restless, giving ourselves both stability and space in which to work with this powerful energy.

Doubt

Both meditation practice and therapy require a measure of faith. From a Buddhist perspective, this doesn't mean blind faith. We're not asked to believe in something because we are told to believe in it. In fact, the Buddha specifically suggests that we don't automatically trust what we are told, even when he is the one telling us! However, we are asked to have faith in the process, I think. The Buddha urged his followers to look deeply into their own experience to decide what was true rather than blindly trusting the opinions or teachings of others. He once came to a town—Kalama—whose residents had been visited by a succession of teachers, each claiming to have true knowledge and teaching while denigrating the teaching of the others gurus who had visited. The residents of Kalama wondered how to make sense of all that they were hearing and how to decide which path to follow. Rather than proclaim his own teachings correct, the Buddha told them:

> Now, Kalamans, don't go by reports, by legends, by traditions, by scripture, by logical conjecture, by inference, by analogies, by agreement through pondering views, by probability, or by the thought, "This contemplative is our teacher." When you know for yourselves that, "These qualities are skillful; these qualities are blameless; these qualities are praised by the wise; these qualities, when adopted and carried out, lead to welfare and to happiness"—then you should enter and remain in them.
>
> (Thera, 2011)

While this initially seems like a sort of "anything goes" prescription, it isn't. Rather, the Buddha suggests that we must test everything in the crucible of our own experience with as pure a mind as we can muster so that we can see clearly the results of our actions and beliefs. Only when we see the results of our actions will we know if we should embrace the qualities or ideas guiding those actions. We aren't being invited to throw out all knowledge that has come before. It is a starting place, but we must also have faith in our own experience and in the process the Buddha describes. And we often must maintain this faith in the midst of ambiguity and uncertainty when it would be much easier to simply accept as true what we are told is true.

Doing therapy also requires faith. We have to have faith in our ability to encounter another person in a helpful way. We have to trust our ability to help the client set a reasonable path and pursue it without getting derailed. We have to trust that we can accurately discern what's happening in front of us and respond to it with skill and wisdom. All of this takes place, for the most part, without clear feedback. Our professional conferences and workshops make me think of the Kalamans, as presenter after presenter will tell us how their model is the ideal one to treat trauma or infidelity or depression. What should we believe? We follow a proven model, but our interventions appear to have no effect at all. Change occurs and it is hard to know to what we should credit it. The same is true of failures. Sometimes clients leave us without a word of explanation and we are left to make our best guess at why.

I once saw a woman in therapy who was living in an incredibly abusive relationship. She was also drinking excessively. Her drinking made sense on one hand because it numbed the pain of the abuse. On the other hand, it made it hard for her to take decisive action to leave her husband and free herself from his frank torture of her. I suggested a number of times that she seek treatment for her drinking and we talked about how it made it hard for her to protect and care for herself. One day, she left a phone message that she wouldn't be coming back. I asked my secretary if she had said why, or given any reason. She hadn't.

I assumed my client had tired of my talking about her drinking or wasn't yet ready to make a change, and had drifted away essentially unhelped. I thought about her from time to time and recalled her stories of how her husband had forced her to have sex with friends and then had beaten her for being with other men. I wondered what had ever become of her.

I lived in a small town at the time and was playing softball in a city league the next summer. One evening my team showed up for a game and discovered we were playing against a team from the local recovery house. Their right fielder was my client! She ran up to me as soon as she saw me.

"You helped me so much," she told me. "I'm sorry I never came back to see you, but I had to sneak away from Ronnie if I was ever going to be free. I've been in AA for months now and I'm living at the recovery house. I even have a new boyfriend."

It was a strong teaching about the degree to which we need to live with "not knowing" in this work, and how seductive it can be to doubt what we do.

In both therapy and mindfulness practice, it is easy for doubt to creep in around the edges of faith. It's tricky because we need a certain amount of doubt. To see the truth for ourselves, as the Buddha suggested to the Kalamans, we need to question what we are taught, test the views of others in the laboratory of our own experience, and not take things at face value. In that sense, doubt is a prized quality. As therapists, we learn to hold what clients say to us gently, knowing that there may be other parts of their experience they aren't yet ready to reveal. We also learn to test the models we are taught in our own experience, taking what we find useful from them without accepting them blindly.

Doubt becomes troublesome when it grows more pervasive. When it operates as a hindrance, it serves more as a defense against the world than as a way of questioning that takes us deeper in our experience. Cynicism seems like such a common stance among therapists, especially as we find what doing therapy is like doesn't match what we hoped it would be. Instead of facing our disappointment and finding a better balance as therapists, it's tempting to doubt the whole enterprise, hiding our sense of failure and vulnerability behind a wall of cynicism. It may mask a sense that we're not good enough, can't do it, are failures at our chosen professions. Or we blame the clients. They don't want help. They have character disorders and you know those people don't change.

Another way that doubt shows up is through indecision. In the grip of doubt, we may find it hard to settle on a meditation practice to delve deeply into. Sometimes this even happens in a single sitting. We start with breath meditation. Nope, that doesn't seem to be doing anything. Let's try lovingkindness meditation. Still nothing? How about a mantra? Moving so quickly in search of the perfect meditation practice means we don't have the time to find the wisdom in any of them. I sometimes find myself doing the same thing in therapy as I switch from approach to approach, searching for the perfect one but not using any to really structure my work in a thoughtful way. Integrating aspects of different models is fine and useful, but when doubt sets in it seems to become reactive, a response to the creeping conviction that I'm not helping, that I'm not doing my client any good.

How do we work skillfully with doubt? Like all the hindrances, we begin by trying to see it clearly. Doubt easily comes to seem all-encompassing. It isn't a quality of our experience; it is fundamental to who we are and we can't imagine ourselves without it. As we recognize that we're in a state of doubt, we can then look more closely to see what might be behind doubt. Often what we find is fear. Fear takes many forms: I can't do this. I'll never get it. I'm not good at meditating. I'll never be the therapist I want to be. I don't deserve the trust of my clients. There's no real relief for my suffering, so why even try?

For me, the antidote to doubt isn't faith as much as it is connection. In my life, doubt becomes isolating. The more absorbed in doubt I become, the less I feel able to reach out to others because to me they all look like things are going great for them. Sometimes we present ourselves that way. And sometimes it's just the way I imagine things to be. Regardless, feeling deficient makes it hard to reach out, even though connection is what I need the most. The Buddha suggested that there are three refuges where we can seek comfort and support when the going gets tough. One of them is the *sangha,* or the community. I know that sitting regularly with others who are pursuing the path of mindfulness energizes my practice and helps keep doubt manageable if not completely at bay. There is a special quality to group mindfulness practice as the quiet holds all of us who have come together. When a group isn't available, I remind myself that the community extends in time and remember the generations of people who have followed this path and found benefit from it. A few years ago, I visited a museum that had an extensive collection of Eastern religious artifacts. In the back of one of the exhibit halls, tucked away nearly out of sight, was a small room with two large statues of the Buddha set in a temple-like display. The room was barely lit and there were benches where one could rest. It was a quiet day at the museum and I decided to take a few moments to meditate. As I sat, watching my breath, I had a vision of all the people who had sat in the presence of these two beautiful statues and it was as if they all gathered around me. It was a powerful experience of the historical community we all join when we begin to explore our experience in a mindful way.

Community is equally important for therapists. I tell my students over and over again that the best way to get in trouble as a therapist is to practice in isolation. I know too many stories of therapists who have ruined their careers or hurt their clients doing things that, I believe, would have immediately seemed unthinkable had they only said them out loud to a trusted colleague. Pick your colleagues carefully. They need to be supportive but willing to give you direct feedback. And they need to recognize the need to struggle against doubt rather than surrender to it. Professional groups can become ways to bond together in cynicism and that does no one any good.

A couple of years ago, I attended a weeklong study retreat. A small group of us studied the classical Buddhist texts in the mornings and then explored the concepts in silent meditation in the afternoon and evening. I struck up an acquaintance with another participant who also taught in a university and trained students to become therapists. I told him that I was teaching mindfulness to the students in our program as they began their clinical practicum.

"I used to do that," he said, "but I finally stopped."

I asked him why since I was really excited about the changes I was seeing in my students and their reports of how useful the practice was.

"First I was teaching them mindfulness and then they were running into problems and so I was teaching them about the hindrances and that wasn't what they needed to learn to be therapists."

I can't say that I feel the same way. Of course, there is much more to being a therapist than being mindful, but what happens in meditation also happens in the rest of life. There are obstacles to being present both as meditators and as therapists and we need to know how to deal with them.

8

PRACTICING TO BE PRESENT

By this time, I have written (and hopefully you have read!), a lot of words about mindfulness and how it can be useful to therapists. As I said at the beginning of the book, however, words aren't the best way to convey the true depth of this practice and the profound effect it can have on our lives, both personal and professional. Experience is the best teacher of mindfulness and to that end, we practice and, as best we can, we practice consistently. Developing a consistent practice requires some supports and I want to suggest some of them to you in this chapter.

The Psychological Container

Mindfulness practice happens in a physical container, of course—a place to meditate, a chair or cushion, an appropriate posture—but it also occurs in an emotional or psychological container. Sometimes it is harder to find a good psychological container for our practice than it is to find a physical one. The psychological container consists of the intention and motivation we bring to our practice as well as the attitudes we have about practice.

"What is my intention for this period of practice?"

This is a question I try to consider each time I make a conscious effort to practice. It serves as a kind of guidepost. Without articulating our intention, practice can start to drift, taking on a rote quality that may look like being present with whatever arises but is dull or unfocused. Remember, as we discussed in an earlier chapter, that an intention is different than a goal. Intentions give us direction and guide us deeper and deeper into a process, but don't define an endpoint that we can reach. "Being present with my experience as best I can" is an example of an intention that we might bring to a period of practice. Being present is an ongoing and ever-unfolding process. "Paying attention to every breath for 5 minutes" is a goal. We can conceivably do it, although we are almost certain to fail at this particular goal. That's where goals become troublesome. Goals define success or failure and once we "fail"—"Oops, where was my mind? I wasn't paying attention to my breath there for a minute"—they invite us to give up on the practice, or blame ourselves: "What's the point? I'll never be any good at this." Intentions, however, create a space that allows us to come back to the practice, knowing that we are deepening the process each time we do. So, think carefully about your intentions and use them to guide but not crush your efforts to practice.

Surrounding each practice session is the larger issue of overall motivation. Why are we engaging in this practice at all? Therapists may have both professional and personal motivations. As therapists, our motivation may be to be more present in the room, to keep ourselves fresh and alive in our work, or to deal better with the stress of doing therapy. At the personal level, our motivation might be to deepen our spiritual presence, to bring more compassion to our lives, or even to deal more effectively with anxiety or depression. It may be an artificial distinction, but I think of intention as what we bring to each practice session and motivation as our overall hopes for the practice.

How important are intention and motivation in developing and sustaining a mindfulness practice? Important. Shapiro (1992) did an interesting study of the trajectories, as it were, of people with long-term meditation practices. Several findings important to our discussion emerged. First, the attitude that long-term meditators brought to their practice was different from the attitudes of those with less experience. Long-term meditators were more likely to look at practice sessions with a positive attitude (glad to be practicing, my time for silence, bringing compassion to myself and others) compared to shorter-term meditators who either weren't aware of the attitude they brought to a session or had mixed or negative expectations (hope I don't have pain, hope nothing difficult comes up today). Also important was the attitude that longer-term meditators had when they *didn't* practice. While shorter-term meditators blamed external conditions (not enough time, no quiet place to sit) or themselves (lazy, no motivation) when they didn't practice, longer-term meditators approached times they didn't practice with curiosity and as an opportunity to learn more about themselves and their practice. Finally, Shapiro found that overall motivation for practice appears to change over time. He calls it the movement from self-regulation to self-exploration to self-liberation. Many people start a meditation practice with a motivation for self-regulation such as stress management or pain control, and then became more interested in simply learning about the habits of the mind or self-exploration and finally became interested in being of service to, or having more compassion for, others, a goal of self-transcendence or liberation. Not everyone makes this progression nor is it necessary that everyone do so. I learned transcendental meditation a few years before I began to practice mindfulness, and I didn't practice it for long. However, during the time I did practice it, I stopped what had been a two-pack-a-day smoking habit. Doing so had a profound impact on my life, even though I wouldn't say I saw my practice as leading to self-exploration per se. So the intentions and motivations we bring to this practice matter and they may likely shift over time.

In addition to intention and motivation, other attitudes can help build and sustain our practice. It helps to take a patient, long-term view of this work. The benefits of practice accrue best over time and with consistent effort. While flashes of insight and truly moving experiences happen, in my experience, the benefits are often more subtle than that and sometimes are only obvious upon reflection. I like to think of Woody Allen's remark that "Eighty percent of success is showing up." Each moment of showing up on the meditation cushion is another part of the whole. Sometimes those moments are profound and sometimes they are seemingly unremarkable, but showing up counts regardless of the content of the moment. You are beginning a path that can provide growth and challenge for a lifetime. Be patient. Remember that this is a journey without an end.

Perfectionism can be a real obstacle to practice and, sadly, one that haunts many of us. The doing mind urges us to "do it right," often with an unclear vision of what "right" is. We find ourselves chasing a goal that we can't really articulate or define, yet we know we're not meeting it and the accompanying judgment becomes discouragement over time, making it hard to even sit down to try to meditate. Accompanying perfectionism is the comparing mind. When we're caught in the midst of thinking we're not doing it right, we seem to see many examples of others who are better than we can ever be. I once sat a 10-day retreat where the problem of comparison was driven home to me. In most retreat settings, you usually find a space to sit and then don't move around much over the course of the retreat. Thus, you end up with "neighbors" who become familiar even though retreat protocol precludes talking or even making eye contact. In this retreat, I sat next to a woman who had the most perfect sitting posture I have ever seen. She easily assumed the cross-legged meditation position on her cushion, let her hands rest effortlessly on her bent knees, and had the most beatific look on her face. While I wasn't staring at her throughout our sits, I was pretty sure she didn't move at all for the 45-minute meditation periods. I, on the other hand, was in hell. I was restless from the start and my restlessness didn't ease much. My back hurt and I kept adjusting how I was sitting to ease the pain. I was awash in emotions generated by a big transition that was going on in my life. None of the peace and self-compassion I was hoping to find seemed available to me. In other words, I felt like a total failure next to the serene young woman sitting next to me. This might have just been another experience of the comparing mind doing its thing, if happenstance hadn't intervened. As sometimes happens at the end of retreats, people need rides to airports and train stations and there is a sign-up board for those who need rides and those who can offer them. I ended up giving my neighbor a ride. We chatted a bit about the retreat.

"I was so intimidated by you," I told her. "Your practice looked so effortless and perfect."

She started giggling. "This was the most difficult retreat I've ever sat. My mind was all over the place. I just broke up with my boyfriend and I was either arguing with him in my mind or trying not to cry. All I could do was sit as still as I could and be present with it."

She was quiet for a moment.

"I have to tell you that I was intimidated by you. You seemed so real and down to earth. I saw you move a couple of times and I could hear the emotion in your breathing once or twice. I wished I could be that real and at ease with the practice. I was afraid if I did, I'd fall apart."

We both began laughing at that point. It was the classic situation of two people imagining the worst about themselves and the best about the other. And it was an important lesson about the amount of energy comparing can use up in the absence of any data.

Another way to build your practice is to not make it too complex. Simplicity can provide a very helpful structure. What do I mean by simplicity? First of all, I have found it useful to pick one practice—for instance, focusing on the sensations of breathing—and sticking with it for a significant period of time. It can be tempting to jump from practice to practice—a little breath focus, a little lovingkindness meditation, some walking meditation, some sound focus, and so forth. In doing so, however, it can be hard to find the gift of each approach and miss the fact that sometimes the simplest approach has the most to offer. Simplicity also means accepting what's right for you at this point in practice. It may be that 15 minutes of practice is right for you at this point even though your friends are sitting for 45 minutes, or sitting twice a day. Of course, there are benefits from extended practice, but practice doesn't need to be long, arduous, and/or complex in order to have benefit. Recall the patient, long-term perspective.

Finally, relax. Don't make meditation another unpleasant or stressful task in the long list of stressful tasks that take up much of our time. See if you can make mindfulness practice a refuge from the ravages of our daily lives that are filled with deadlines, judgments, measures of success, and the many, many seductions of multitasking. Enjoy your practice as best you can. Appreciate the moments of peace it can provide. And recognize the enormous effort toward changing your life that you are making by simply showing up on the meditation cushion again and again.

Preparing for Practice

A few brief words about preparing for practice. It's generally useful to begin with a specific amount of time you plan to spend meditating. Remember to stay simple; don't become too ambitious right off the bat. Begin with 5 or 10 minutes of practice if that seems manageable. Judgment creeps in so quickly that setting out to sit for a longer time than is reasonably attainable may just be setting yourself up to become discouraged. You will have plenty of time to extend your practice. Start with what you can start with and build from there. My students often find it helpful initially to use a guided meditation soundtrack to help them in the early stages of their practice. As seemingly simple as the instructions for the practice are, prompts from a soundtrack can be very useful. What my students report is that they use the soundtrack for a while and then they begin to feel that it interferes with their practice and they become impatient with it. At that point, they turn to a simple timer or a soundtrack that has bells at regular intervals. It seems a wise use of a support for practice—using it while it proves beneficial but not becoming attached to it that you can't put it aside when its usefulness fades.

Many people find it helpful to have a specific place that they dedicate to meditation practice. As your practice strengthens, it will become possible to meditate in almost any circumstances, but at the beginning you may want to shelter your practice a bit. It's helpful to practice in a place that is relatively quiet, a place where you won't be easily interrupted, and a place that won't distract you. Early on, I tried to meditate in my study at home. While it was quiet and my wife was good about not interrupting, I found it hard to step out of the task-oriented atmosphere of my study. I'd find my mind wandering to the to-do list scrawled on a yellow post-it note and stuck to the edge of my computer screen. If I forgot to turn down the sound on my computer, I could hear the ping of an incoming e-mail and that invited all sorts of distracting thoughts. Once in a while, the pull of a task would be so strong that I would finally get up from my cushion and jot down a note to myself to take care of something when I was done. Needless to say, this setting didn't support my practice well.

Finally, posture. In the traditional Buddhist literature there are four meditation postures—sitting, standing, lying down, and walking. I'll describe walking meditation in a moment. Meditating lying down is quite a challenge for most of us. We're generally so tired that lying down and slowing down at the same time leads right to sleep. While it can be nice to relax into sleep by lying down and focusing on the breath, this can also create an association between meditation and sleep that can be hard to break. I've found it helpful to use a technique like progressive relaxation to help me fall asleep rather than relying on mindfulness practice. That said, meditating while lying prone isn't impossible, and can be a useful way to pay attention to body sensations.

Standing meditation can actually be a good way to meditate when we're feeling sleepy. Sitting or lying down postures allow the body to relax more than standing postures do, so it is not uncommon to see people on retreat standing for part or all of a meditation period if they are struggling with sleepiness. I find a variation of the yoga posture known as *tadasana* or mountain pose works well for me for standing meditation. Stand with the feet approximately shoulder distance apart and with the big toes parallel to each other, bringing a slight inward angle to the feet. As you come into this pose, you might try swaying a bit from side to side to feel your way into it and also to see that you are distributing your weight evenly on the feet, not leaning forward or back or putting more weight on one leg or the other. Align the body over the feet with the center of your head over the center of the pelvis. Raise your head so the bottom of your chin is parallel to the floor, and let your throat relax and tongue soften. Check your shoulders to see if they are relaxed or if they are hunched up toward your ears. Let your shoulder blades slide down your back and lift the chest a bit. Finally, let your arms come to rest beside your body without effort. In this pose, you can easily become aware of the aliveness of the body. The slight adjustments in posture that comprise "standing still" may come into awareness, as may the variety of tingling, moving, and stretching sensations that flow throughout the body. You can also notice how tempting it is to move in this posture. We often tend not to stand for long periods of time without standing being the prelude to walking somewhere. Simply observe and investigate the temptation to move and any reactions that arise to standing.

Sitting meditation posture can be accomplished in a number of ways. The most basic posture is sitting in a chair and it is a good posture for many of us who don't have the flexibility to sit in a cross-legged or kneeling position on the floor. The best chair for sitting meditation is one that has a relatively straight back and a firm seat that will support you comfortably. Chairs that invite you to recline or hunch over may not be as useful. Sit with both feet comfortably on the ground. (I realize that chairs don't fit well for some people. You can use a blanket or cushion on the floor to support your feet if the chair seat is too high for you to comfortably have your feet on the ground.) Keep your back as straight as you can without straining. The primary consideration is letting the breath come easily and naturally, so you should not be straining to sit up too straight, nor should you be hunching over or collapsing into the back of the chair. If your back needs a bit of support, rest it gently against the chair back. If doing so makes it hard to breathe easily, you might want to find a different chair. Let your hands rest on your thighs or in your lap. Your posture should comfortably support the body while letting you breathe unimpeded. Most of us find it helpful to close our eyes while meditating, but it isn't absolutely necessary. If you close your eyes, you can raise your head as if you are looking straight out at the horizon. If you keep your eyes open, let your gaze drift down to a place on the floor a few feet in front of you and let your gaze grow soft. This isn't the time to admire the pattern in the carpet or count the dust bunnies that you need to clean up from underneath the furniture. It's important to recognize that, for some people, closing the eyes can be anxiety provoking. Take care of yourself in this process and attend to what works best for you. If you decide to use a meditation cushion or bench for sitting meditation, I think it's best to get specific instruction in what postures work best with them. Because most of us are not used to sitting for extended periods in either position required by a cushion or a bench, getting used to them takes time and some instruction.

The Active Mind

One of the first things I hear from many of my students when I introduce them to mindfulness practice is some version of this:

"I can't meditate. My mind is always going 90 miles an hour and it won't slow down."

While it's common for graduate students to experience this—active minds are what got them into graduate school, after all, and the work of graduate school invites a lot of mind activity—it isn't limited to students. Unless we're living in a monastery or another protected space specifically designed to help us profoundly slow down and focus on our experience, our minds remain quite active. There's nothing wrong with an active mind, of course, and part of the work of mindfulness practice is to observe that mental activity, and to do our best to bring compassion and understanding to it, without trying to make it different. There are times, however, when the mind is so active that it seems nearly impossible to have even a little bit of focus on the breath. At a certain point, the struggle becomes overwhelming and we are tempted to simply give up. That's when some other ways to work with the restless and active mind can be useful.

Recall that, earlier in this chapter, I said there are four classic postures for meditation, one of which is walking meditation. Walking meditation uses the physical sensations of walking as the anchor, like sitting meditation often uses the breath. Walking meditation can be a useful practice when the mind or body is so restless and full of energy that it is difficult to be still. Alternatively, it can also be a useful practice when we're tired or sleepy. In other words, it can help to regulate our energy level. Finally, the formal practice of walking meditation can provide the basis for walking in everyday life to have a meditative aspect. A walk down the hall to the drinking fountain can be a moment of presence that brings the mind back from wherever it may have gone in the midst of a busy day. Mindful walking is a true meditation practice; there is nothing second-best about it. In fact, one of my teachers said that the last of the Buddha's students to achieve enlightenment while the historical Buddha was alive did so while engaged in walking meditation.

The formal practice of walking meditation begins with finding a space in which to walk where you won't be too distracted, nor too self-conscious from others being around. Formal walking practice can look a bit strange since we will slow down the process of walking considerably in order to pay close attention to the physical sensations of moving the body through the world. Find a place where you can walk back and forth in a "lane," taking 10 to 12 steps before you need to stop and turn around. To give you an idea of the kind of space that works best, one of the most unique places I have ever practiced walking meditation is on a one-lane bowling alley in the basement of the Insight Meditation Society main hall in Massachusetts. The bowling alley was built by some previous owner of the building, but it was perfect for walking meditation with two people using it at a time, since about half the length of the alley was the right distance for walking.

Start by simply standing still, in the standing meditation position I described above, and bringing your attention to all of the body sensations as they arise. For most of us, standing still is not standing without motion. The body is constantly making small adjustments in order to stay upright. We shift weight slightly from foot to foot, the body sways a bit, the chest and belly still move with the movement of the breath. "Still" is a relative term! As your attention pulls away from the outside world a bit and focuses on the body, set an intention to pay attention to the sensations of walking as best you can. When you feel ready, slowly lift one foot, feeling each small movement that goes into lifting the foot. I like to see if I can sense the very last bit of contact the foot has with the ground before it is completely in the air. Then bring your attention to moving the foot forward, still in the air, sensing all the muscles moving, the feeling of the foot no longer in contact with the ground, how the body reacts and adjusts to the lack of stability resulting from only one foot on the ground. Finally, complete this first step by placing the foot ahead on the ground, trying to feel the first contact with the floor; and then sustain your attention as the foot makes complete contact, feeling the spread of the foot as more weight is transferred from the back foot to the now front foot and the process begins again. Continue walking, and paying attention to the sensations of moving, until you come to the end of your walking space. At this point, stand for a moment, becoming aware of all the sensations in the body as forward movement stops and the body comes to rest. Then, slowly turn around, paying careful attention to the movements of turning, noticing how the body shifts your weight from one foot to the other as you turn. Finally, when you have turned to face back the way you came, begin to walk back, paying attention to the sensations of walking. This practice is helped by walking more slowly than you usually would walk. In fact, it's helpful to walk *much* more slowly. Slowing down the movements makes it easier to really focus on them, although it can also result in you feeling a bit awkward and off balance. You can also feel a bit self-conscious walking so slowly, and that's why a private space may be a good place to practice where you won't be observed by others. I have to admit that walking meditation can look really silly. I once remember sitting up on the broad veranda of a meditation hall while dozens of people practiced walking meditation on the large lawn in front of the building. Had I not known better, I would have thought that zombies had invaded and decided to come to the meditation retreat! As you become more experienced at mindful walking, you may decide to speed up your pace a bit, but remember that the point of walking meditation is not to get somewhere. The point is to be present with what is happening in the present moment. Don't close your eyes during walking meditation since you need to see where you are going, especially if you are sharing the walking space with others.

As happens during breath meditation, you will find your attention drawn away from the sensations of walking from time to time. You may become interested in something you see in the environment. You may become lost in thought. Whatever the reason, the process is the same. When you notice that you are no longer paying attention to the sensations of walking, then (as best you can) release whatever has captured your attention, and with kindness bring your attention back to the process of one step following another as you move through space. If you find yourself really distracted or agitated, you can stop at any time to stand for a moment, getting in touch with the breath and with the sensation of the whole body standing. When you have reestablished a more centered presence, resume mindful walking.

As you gain experience with the formal practice of walking meditation, you can begin to bring some of the same attention to walking in daily life. Of course, you don't want to walk slowly down the aisles of the grocery store, leading other customers to think you actually are a zombie. However, you can pay attention to the contact of your feet on the floor, the movement of the feet and legs as you walk at a comfortable pace, the movement of the air across the body as you walk, and so on. Doing so can both begin to bring the concentration and awareness developed in formal practice into daily life and can provide moments of peace and focus in the midst of an otherwise busy day.

While walking meditation can be one way to practice when the mind is agitated, it isn't always available. You may not find yourself in a circumstance where you can walk, or it might not be appropriate to do so. Another means to deal with a busy mind that I find useful is counting breaths. I think of it as giving the mind a job to do that can occupy and calm it. Breath counting is easily explained, although oftentimes challenging in practice. Just as in regular breath meditation, the anchor is the physical sensation of breathing. However, in addition to feeling the rise and fall of the chest, or the movement of the air at the nostrils, part of the mind also silently counts breaths, beginning with one and counting until the tenth breath, at which point you start over again. As always happens, you will find yourself distracted and when you realize that you have lost count, simply start over again at "one." I find it useful to count on the exhalation and then let the breath simply rest when the exhalation stops, waiting for the next breath to arise. There is a moment of lovely calm between breaths that we can rest in before the next breath arises on its own. When the mind is agitated and seems to be clinging to doing mode, breath counting can be a way for the mind to do something without completely interfering with practice. Many of my students find it a useful way to practice in the midst of an agitated mind. Be forewarned that there is plenty of room for self-judgment in this practice and it is tempting to beat yourself up for not reaching "ten" consistently. As always happens, the habits of the mind quickly point us toward goals and doing, and without some vigilance, we soon think we are failing and begin beating ourselves up for doing so. This practice depends on compassion just as much as any other mindfulness practice.

Finally, it is possible to bring mindful awareness to everyday activities. As with walking meditation, doing so helps to bring the awareness arising from formal practice into the everyday world. It can also be a way to cultivate some mindfulness in the midst of a busy life and a busy mind. We spend much of our waking day not really engaged with the activities in which we are involved. Think back to the last meal you ate. Can you recall what you ate? Can you remember the experience of eating it, the aroma of the food, the sensations of chewing and swallowing, the texture of the food, or even the conversation you might have had if you ate with another person? Where was your mind during the drive to or from work, or while you were doing housework, or walking the dog? We can use any of these activities as ways to practice. As with any other mindfulness practice, mindfulness of everyday activities begins with a pause and a step outside of our habitual autopilot mode. We set the intention to bring gentle yet careful awareness to the activity in which we are about to engage. We investigate the three components of experience as they manifest themselves in the activity; what physical action and stimuli do we encounter, what thoughts accompany the activity, what is the emotion tone? We can also pay attention to distraction as it takes us away from the moment-to-moment awareness of what we are doing and leads us into the past or the future or into judgment. It can be instructive to bring this kind of awareness to relatively mundane activities because they will often blossom into intriguing experiences when we do so. The grape-eating exercise earlier in the book is one example. But let's take another example. What would it be like to bring mindful awareness to the act of taking a shower?

Begin by stepping out of the routine of showering. Pause for a moment and set the intention to really pay attention this time to the experience of taking a shower. Open the door to the shower stall and turn on the water, listening to the water flow out through the shower head and splash against the wall. As you undress, feel the sensation of your clothes against your skin and the exposure to the air when you are no longer clothed. Notice the sensation of the floor or the rug or bath mat against your bare feet—the smell of the water as you enter the shower—the first sense of temperature and sensation as the water hits the skin. Pay attention to thoughts and judgments as well. Does the mind tell you that this is silly and a waste of time? Do you have feelings or judgments about your body? Notice the difference in sensation between the parts of the body that are under the stream of the shower and those that aren't. Feel how the hand glides over the skin as you apply soap. Notice the aroma of the soap. Watch the suds on the floor of the shower. Maintain your awareness as you rinse and shut off the shower. Notice what a different sensation the towel is as you begin to dry yourself. Pay attention to temperature as you leave the warmth of the shower stall into the cool air outside.

We can bring mindfulness to any number of everyday activities: doing the dishes, loading or unloading the dishwasher, sweeping the floor, making the bed, walking to get the mail. Mindfulness is a way to anchor ourselves in the present moment and step out of the mind's narratives that usually keep us far from what is happening right in front of us. And that far place is often a scarier place than the moment that is here now.

9

A FINAL THOUGHT

It always catches me off guard in early December when the sun sets in late afternoon. It doesn't seem like I should be going home from work in the dark. I like the last few moments in the office at the end of the day. Today has been a busy one. I supervised a couple of students, taught a seminar, took care of some administrative tasks, and saw three clients. It's the kind of day I like—full of variety and activity. Now, with people leaving or gone, it's quiet and I have a few moments to think over what I've done and do anything that I need to do to get ready for tomorrow. Of all the things that I do, my thoughts almost always gravitate, at the end of the day, to my clients.

My first client was a woman I've seen for eight sessions now and her therapy is flowing along smoothly. We seem to be in sync and she is willing to try what I suggest in the session, going inside to examine some of her beliefs about herself that emerged from a childhood filled with deprivation and emotional danger. The work seems effortless. It is the kind of work that therapists—or this therapist, at least—generally dream of. I feel like I am right there with her as we work, my mind rarely wandering from what is happening in the room.

My second client was more of a challenge. I've also seen her for about eight sessions, but we don't seem to have really connected yet. She comes dutifully and talks candidly about her life, but there is a barely perceptible wall between us. As she talks about the difficulties of her life, I find myself removed a bit, even at times impatient. It doesn't seem like we're getting to the work that needs to be done. I struggle to stay present, grounding myself with my breath and with the awareness that, for right now, maybe I don't need to *do* anything, just be with her in the way she needs to be with me. I know enough of her past to realize that trusting someone, wanting something from a relationship, even a professional therapeutic relationship, could be terrifying. I remember the hindrances and how they operate in therapy. I'm grasping for something and that usually means I'm struggling with an underlying wish to control things that I can't control. Today I tried my best to soften into the session. I'm not sure how successful I was.

My third client scares me. He doesn't threaten me physically, but there is a strong part of him that is seriously wondering if continuing to live makes sense. I want to keep my distance from that part. Given his heavy drinking that both numbs and then fuels his despair, I want nothing more than to ship him off to rehab. It may be the right thing to do and it may be the right thing to do soon, but I don't want to do it because I'm afraid. I think my client can feel that fear, and my suggestions that he consider substance abuse treatment seem not to register.

"I don't know what that would look like, not drinking," is all he can say.

I sit with him, doing my best not to emotionally run away, watching my breath and sometimes even grounding myself by just trying to feel my feet on the floor. I trust that the less I act from fear, the more chance I have of reaching him, but it's hard. The hours I spend with him are among the most difficult therapy hours I've experienced in a long time. I'm hoping that the antidepressant his psychiatrist has prescribed will start to work, but I know his alcohol consumption is interfering with the medication. Consequently, mixed with the fear is a bit of anger.

"Why are you doing this to me?" I want to say to him. "Why are you making me feel things I don't want to feel?"

And that's how it goes most days. I've been practicing mindfulness for a long time now and I've been teaching it to my students and to an occasional client for a while now, too. I've given talks about the usefulness of the practice all over the country and in Europe as well. You'd think I wouldn't struggle so much. But I do. And yet I don't. Mindfulness isn't a miracle cure. Practicing mindfulness doesn't relieve us of being human, with all the fears and anxieties and uncertainties that come with our humanity. It doesn't make us perfect therapists or perfect partners or perfect parents or perfect anything. I think that's important to know. Mindfulness is a journey. I think it's a necessary journey for therapists and I think it can make radical changes in our lives. I know it has made changes in mine. But at the end of the day we must come bearing compassion, too. We must be ready to forgive ourselves over and over again. My intention, borne of years of practice, is to bring presence and depth to each experience in my life, to each client encounter. Some days, I fall asleep satisfied with my efforts. On other days, I realize all I can do is breathe and show up again the next day, ready to try again. What my mindfulness practice has done for me is to give me more patience with this process, more equanimity with the ebb and flow of life. At least that's true most days. Other days I practice mindlessness like a pro!

REFERENCES

Ashforth, B. E., & Humphrey, R. H. (1993). Emotional Labor in Service Roles: The Influence of Identity. *Academy of Management Review, 18*(1), 88. doi:10.2307/258824

Baer, R. A. (2003). Mindfulness Training as a Clinical Intervention: A Conceptual and Empirical Review. *Clinical Psychology: Science and Practice, 10*(2), 125–143. doi:10.1093/clipsy/bpg015

Baker, E. K. (2003). *Caring for ourselves: A therapist's guide to personal and professional well-being.* Washington, DC: American Psychological Association.

Barnes, S., Brown, K. W., Krusemark, E., Campbell, W. K., & Rogge, R. D. (2007). The Role of Mindfulness in Romantic Relationship Satisfaction and Responses to Relationship Stress. *Journal of Marital and Family Therapy, 33*(4), 482–500. doi:10.1111/j.1752-0606.2007.00033.x

Beddoe, A. E., & Murphy, S. O. (2004). Does Mindfulness Decrease Stress and Foster Empathy Among Nursing Students? *Journal of Nursing Education, 43*(7), 305–312.

Brotheridge, C. M., & Grandey, A. A. (2002). Emotional Labor and Burnout: Comparing Two Perspectives of "People Work." *Journal of Vocational Behavior, 60*(1), 17–39. doi:10.1006/jvbe.2001.1815

Brown, K. W., & Ryan, R. M. (2003). The Benefits of Being Present: Mindfulness and Its Role in Psychological Well-Being. *Journal of Personality and Social Psychology, 84*(4), 822–848. doi:10.1037/0022-3514.84.4.822

Centers for Disease Control. (2013). Insufficient sleep is a public health epidemic. Retrieved from www.cdc.gov/features/dssleep/

Chambers, R., Lo, B. C. Y., & Allen, N. B. (2007). The Impact of Intensive Mindfulness Training on Attentional Control, Cognitive Style, and Affect. *Cognitive Therapy and Research, 32*(3), 303–322. doi:10.1007/s10608-007-9119-0

Chiesa, A., & Serretti, A. (2009). Mindfulness-Based Stress Reduction for Stress Management in Healthy People: A Review and Meta-Analysis. *Journal of Alternative and Complementary Medicine, 15*(5), 593–600. doi:10.1089/acm.2008.0495

Cohen-Katz, J., Wiley, S., Capuano, T., Baker, D. M., Deitrick, L., & Shapiro, S. L. (2005). The Effects of Mindfulness-Based Stress Reduction on Nurse Stress and Burnout: A Qualitative and Quantitative Study, Part II. *Holistic Nursing Practice, 19*(2), 78–86. Retrieved from www.ncbi.nlm.nih.gov/pubmed/15871591

95

Cullen, M. (2011). Mindfulness-Based Interventions: An Emerging Phenomenon. *Mindfulness, 2*(3), 186–193. doi:10.1007/s12671-011-0058-1

Dyregrov, K. (2003). Micro-Sociological Analysis of Social Support Following Traumatic Bereavement: Unhelpful and Avoidant Responses From the Community. *OMEGA—Journal of Death and Dying, 48*(1), 23–44. doi:10.2190/T3NM-VFBK-68R0-UJ60

Escuriex, B. F., & Labbé, E. E. (2011). Health Care Providers' Mindfulness and Treatment Outcomes: A Critical Review of the Research Literature. *Mindfulness, 2*(4), 242–253. doi:10.1007/s12671-011-0068-z

Figley, C. R. (Ed.). (2002). *Treating compassion fatigue.* New York, NY: Routledge.

Gehart, D. R., & McCollum, E. E. (2007). Engaging Suffering: Towards a Mindful Re-Visioning of Family Therapy Practice. *Journal of Marital and Family Therapy, 33*(2), 214–226.

Geller, S. M., & Greenberg, L. S. (2002). Therapeutic Presence: Therapists' Experience of Presence in the Psychotherapy Encounter. *Person-Centered and Experiential Psychotherapies, 1,* 71–86.

Germer, C. K. (2009). *The mindful path to self-compassion: Freeing yourself from destructive thoughts and emotions.* New York: Guilford Press.

Gilbert, P. (2009). *Compassionate mind: A new approach to life's challenges.* London: Constable & Robinson.

Gilbert, P. (2010). *Compassion focused therapy: Distinctive features.* New York, NY: Routledge.

Gilbert, P., McEwan, K., Matos, M., & Rivis, A. (2011). Fears of Compassion: Development of Three Self-Report Measures. *Psychology and Psychotherapy, 84*(3), 239–255. doi:10.1348/147608310X526511

Grepmair, L., Mitterlehner, F., Loew, T., Bachler, E., Rother, W., & Nickel, M. (2007). Promoting Mindfulness in Psychotherapists in Training Influences the Treatment Results of Their Patients: A Randomized, Double-Blind, Controlled Study. *Psychotherapy and Psychosomatics, 76*(6), 332–338. doi:10.1159/000107560

Hanson, R., & Mendius, R. (2009). *Buddha's brain: The practical neuroscience of happiness, love and wisdom.* Oakland, CA: New Harbinger.

Harrison, R. L., & Westwood, M. T. (2009). Preventing Vicarious Victimization of Mental Health Therapists: Identifying Protective Practices. *Psychotherapy Theory Research Practice Training, 46,* 203–219.

Hassed, C., de Lisle, S., Sullivan, G., & Pier, C. (2009). Enhancing the Health of Medical Students: Outcomes of an Integrated Mindfulness and Lifestyle Program. *Advances in Health Sciences Education: Theory and Practice, 14*(3), 387–398. doi:10.1007/s10459-008-9125-3

Hayes, S. C. (2003). Buddhism and Acceptance and Commitment Therapy. *Cognitive and Behavioral Practice, 9*(1), 58–66.

Hayes, S. C., Strosahl, K. D., & Wilson, K. G. (2011). *Acceptance and commitment therapy: The process and practice of mindful change* (2nd ed.). New York, NY: Guildford Press.

Hochschild, A. R. (1983). *The managed heart: Commercialization of human feeling.* Berkeley, CA: University of California Press.

Hofmann, S., & Sawyer, A. (2010). The effect of mindfulness-based therapy on anxiety and depression: A meta-analytic review. *Journal of Consulting and Clinical Psychology, 78*(2), 169–183. doi:10.1037/a0018555

Ingram, K., Betz, N., & Mindes, E. (2001). Unsupportive Responses From Others Concerning a Stressful Life Event: Development of the Unsupportive Social Interactions Inventory. *Journal of Social and and Clinical Psychology, 20*(2), 173–207. doi:10.1521/jscp.20.2.173.22265

James, N. (1989). Emotional Labour: Skill and Work in the Social Regulation of Feelings. *Sociological Review, 37,* 15–42.

Jha, A. P., Stanley, E., Kiyonaga, A., Wong, L., & Gelfand, L. (2010). Examining the Protective Effects of Mindfulness Training on Working Memory Capacity and Affective Experience. *Emotion, 10*(1), 54–64. doi:10.1037/a0018438

Kabat-Zinn, J. (1990). *Full catastrophe living: Using the wisdom of your body and mind to face stress, pain and illness.* New York, NY: Delacorte.

Kabat-Zinn, J., Wheeler, E., Light, T., Skillings, A., Scharf, M. J., Cropley, T. G., . . . Bernhard, J. D. (1998). Influence of a Mindfulness Meditation-Based Stress Reduction Intervention on Rates of Skin Clearing in Patients With Moderate to Severe Psoriasis Undergoing Phototherapy (UVB) and Photochemotherapy (PUVA). *Psychosomatic Medicine, 60*(5), 625–632. Retrieved from www.ncbi.nlm.nih.gov/pubmed/9773769

Khoury, B., Lecomte, T., Fortin, G., Masse, M., Therien, P., Bouchard, V., . . . Hofmann, S. G. (2013). Mindfulness-Based Therapy: A Comprehensive Meta-Analysis. *Clinical Psychology Review, 33*(6), 763–771. doi:10.1016/j.cpr.2013.05.005

Linehan, M. M. (1993). *Cognitive-behavioral treatment of borderline personality disorder.* New York, NY: Guilford Press.

Lovell, J. (2013). George Saunders's Advice to Graduates. *New York Times Magazine.* Retrieved from http://6thfloor.blogs.nytimes.com/2013/07/31/george-saunderss-advice-to-graduates/?_r=0

MacBeth, A., & Gumley, A. (2012). Exploring Compassion: A Meta-Analysis of the Association Between Self-Compassion and Psychopathology. *Clinical Psychology Review, 32*(6), 545–552. doi:10.1016/j.cpr.2012.06.003

McCann, I. L., & Pearlman, L. A. (1990). Vicarious Traumatization: A Framework for Understanding the Psychological Effects of Working With Victims. *Journal of Traumatic Stress, 3*(1), 131–149. Retrieved from www.springerlink.com/index/N25210478583H48R.pdf

McCollum, E. E., & Gehart, D. R. (2010). Using Mindfulness Meditation to Teach Beginning Therapists Therapeutic Presence: A Qualitative Study. *Journal of Marital and Family Therapy, 36,* 347–360. doi:10.1111/j.1752-0606.2010.00214.x

Mann, S. (2004). "People-Work": Emotion Management, Stress and Coping. *British Journal of Guidance & Counselling, 32*(2), 205–221. doi:10.1080/03698 80410001692247

Minor, H. G., Carlson, L. E., MacKenzie, M. J., Zernicke, K., & Jones, L. (2006). Evaluation of a Mindfulness-Based Stress Reduction (MBSR) Program for Caregivers of Children With Chronic Conditions. *Social Work in Health Care, 43*(1), 91–109. doi:10.1300/J010v43n01

Moore, A., & Malinowski, P. (2009). Meditation, Mindfulness and Cognitive Flexibility. *Consciousness and Cognition, 18*(1), 176–186. doi:10.1016/j.concog.2008.12.008

Neff, K. D. (2009). Self-compassion: A healthier way of relating to yourself. Retrieved from www.self-compassion.org/what-is-self-compassion/self-compassion-versus-self-esteem.html

Neff, K. D., Kirkpatrick, K. L., & Rude, S. S. (2007). Self-Compassion and Adaptive Psychological Functioning. *Journal of Research in Personality,* 41(1), 139–154. doi:10.1016/j.jrp.2006.03.004

Norcross, J. C., Pfund, R. A., & Prochaska, J. O. (2013). Psychotherapy in 2022: A Delphi Poll on Its Future. *Professional Psychology: Research and Practice,* 44(5), 363–370. doi:10.1037/a0034633

Ortner, C. N. M., Kilner, S. J., & Zelazo, P. D. (2007). Mindfulness Meditation and Reduced Emotional Interference on a Cognitive Task. *Motivation and Emotion,* 31(4), 271–283. doi:10.1007/s11031-007-9076-7

Parker-Pope, T. (2011). Go easy on yourself, a new wave of research urges. *New York Times Wellness Blog.* Retrieved from http://well.blogs.nytimes.com/2011/02/28/go-easy-on-yourself-a-new-wave-of-research-urges/?_r=0

Praissman, S. (2008). Mindfulness-Based Stress Reduction: A Literature Review and Clinician's Guide. *Journal of the American Academy of Nurse Practitioners,* 20(4), 212–216. doi:10.1111/j.1745-7599.2008.00306.x

Radeke, J. T., & Mahoney, M. J. (2000). Comparing the Personal Lives of Psychotherapists and Research Psychologists. *Professional Psychology: Research and Practice,* 31(1), 82–84. doi:10.1037//0735-7028.31.1.82

Rogers, C. (1957). The Necessary and Sufficient Conditions of Therapeutic Personality Change. *Journal of Consulting Psychology, 21,* 95–103. doi:10.1037/h0045357

Rønnestad, M. H., & Skovholt, T. M. (2003). The Journey of the Counselor and Therapist: Research Findings and Perspectives on Professional Development. *Journal of Career Development, 30*(1), 5–44.

Rosenberg, T., & Pace, M. (2006). Burnout Among Mental Health Professionals: Special Considerations for the Marriage and Family Therapist. *Journal of Marital and Family Therapy, 32*(1), 87–99. Retrieved from www.ncbi.nlm.nih.gov/pubmed/16468683

Rosenzweig, S., Reibel, D. K., Greeson, J. M., Brainard, G. C., & Hojat, M. (2003). Mindfulness-Based Stress Reduction Lowers Psychological Distress in Medical Students. *Teaching and Learning in Medicine, 15*(2), 88–92. doi:10.1207/S15328015TLM1502_03

Sedlmeier, P., Eberth, J., Schwarz, M., Zimmermann, D., Haarig, F., Jaeger, S., & Kunze, S. (2012). The Psychological Effects of Meditation: A Meta-analysis. *Psychological Bulletin, 138*(6), 1139–1171. doi:10.1037/a0028168

Segal, Z. (2008). Finding Daylight: Mindful Recovery From Depression. *Psychotherapy Networker* (January/February), 1–6. Retrieved from http://sfmindfulness.com/Psychotherapy_Networker.pdf

Segal, Z. V., Williams, J. M. G., & Teasdale, J. D. (2002). *Mindfulness-based cognitive therapy for depression: A new approach to preventing relapse.* New York, NY: Guilford Press.

Shapiro, D. H. (1992). A Preliminary Study of Long-Term Meditators: Goals, Effects, Religious Orientation, Cognitions. *Journal of Transpersonal Psychology, 24*(1), 23–39.

Shapiro, S. L., Astin, J. A., Bishop, S. R., & Cordova, M. (2005). Mindfulness-Based Stress Reduction for Health Care Professionals: Results From a Randomized Trial. *International Journal of Stress Management, 12*(2), 164–176.

Shapiro, S. L., Brown, K. W., & Biegel, G. M. (2007). Teaching Self-Care to Caregivers: Effects of Mindfulness-Based Stress Reduction on the Mental Health of Therapists in Training. *Training and Education in Professional Psychology,* *1*(2), 105–115. doi:10.1037/1931-3918.1.2.105

Shapiro, S. L., Schwartz, G. E., & Bonner, G. (1998). Effects of Mindfulness-Based Stress Reduction on Medical and Premedical Students. *Journal of Behavioral Medicine, 21*(6), 581–599. Retrieved from www.ncbi.nlm.nih.gov/pubmed/9891256

Skovholt, T., & Rønnestad, M. (2003). Struggles of the Novice Counselor and Therapist. *Journal of Career Development, 30*(1), 45–58. doi:10.1177/0894845 30303000103

Thera, S. (trans). (2011). Kalama Sutta: The instruction to the Kalamas (AN3.65). Access to Insight. Retrieved from www.accesstoinsight.org/tipitaka/an/an03/an03.065.soma.html

Toller, P. (2011). Bereaved Parents' Experiences of Supportive and Unsupportive Communication. *Southern Communication Journal, 76*(1), 17–34. doi:10.1080/10417940903159393

Tricycle (Producer). (2011, April 4). The five hindrances [Video file]. Retrieved from www.tricycle.com/online-retreats/five-hindrances

Vachon, M. L. S., & Stylianos, S. K. (1988). The Role of Social Support in Bereavement. *Journal of Social Issues, 44*(3), 175–190. doi:10.1111/j.1540-4560.1988.tb02084.x

Wachs, K., & Cordova, J. V. (2007). Mindful Relating: Exploring Mindfulness and Emotion Repertoires in Intimate Relationships. *Journal of Marital and Family Therapy, 33*(4), 464–481. doi:10.1111/j.1752-0606.2007.00032.x

INDEX

RESOURCES

The soundtracks that accompany the exercises in the book can be down-
loaded from the book's website at: http://www.routledgementalhealth.com/
9781138805873/

Open the tab titled "eResources" and you will find the soundtracks. You
can listen to them directly from the website or download them by right-
clicking on the soundtrack title.